"Emily DeArdo li
book will help you

MW01093765

Senior fellow at the National Review Institute

"In *Living Memento Mori*, Emily DeArdo imparts the valuable lessons she has learned while suffering with Jesus by her side. Like the precious drops of Jesus' blood that spattered the Via Dolorosa, DeArdo shares valuable jewels of wisdom gleaned from a life lived in the shadow of death, a memento mori that has brought her closer to our Savior."

From the foreword by **Sr. Theresa Aletheia Noble, F.S.P.**
Author of *Remember Your Death: Memento Mori Lenten Devotional*

"This richly layered book brought me to a new appreciation for the Stations of the Cross and a new understanding of the redemptive value of suffering. While the story is a page-turner, it is also a book to be read slowly and contemplatively, to revisit again and again. Emily DeArdo's life is a testimony to God's graciousness. Her willingness to bear witness to some of humankind's most objectively vulnerable moments is an extraordinary gift of grace to her readers. If you have the courage to take an honest look at the nearness of death and the true gift of every day we live, this skillfully crafted volume can be a beautiful, life-changing instrument."

Elizabeth Foss
Catholic author and founder of *Take Up and Read*

"In my own life, I have found the practice of memento mori and the spirituality of the Stations of the Cross to be places of peace and consolation in the midst of personal suffering and darkness. In *Living Memento Mori*, Emily DeArdo shares her own journey, her own pain, her own need to face the reality of death, and shows us that, hidden in the wounds of Christ, we are never alone."

Tommy Tighe
Author of *The Catholic Hipster Handbook*

"Suffering and death are not easy subjects to meditate on, but in *Living Memento Mori*, Emily DeArdo challenges us to think of our own suffering and inevitable death in a way that brings both wisdom and joy. The honest story of her daily struggle to live with a fatal diagnosis is compelling on its own, but when joined with her unique interpretation of the Stations of the Cross, DeArdo provides a powerful reminder to live each day as if it's our last and gives readers the courage to embrace our crosses and draw closer to Christ."

Mary Lenaburg
Author of *Be Brave in the Scared*

LIVING MEMENTO MORI

My Journey through the Stations of the Cross

Emily M. DeArdo

AVE MARIA PRESS AVE Notre Dame, Indiana

Unless otherwise noted, scripture quotations are from *New Revised Standard Version Bible*, copyright © 1989 National Council of the Churches of Christ in the United States of America. Used by permission. All rights reserved.

Excerpts from *Salvifici Doloris* are copyright © 1984 Libreria Editrice Vaticana. Used by permission.

Foreword © 2019 by Theresa Aletheia Noble, F.S.P.

Founded in 1865, Ave Maria Press is a ministry of the United States Province of Holy Cross.

www.avemariapress.com

Paperback: ISBN-13 978-1-59471-967-7

E-book: ISBN-13 978-1-59471-968-4

Cover image © Westend61/GettyImages.com.

Cover and text design by Samantha Watson.

Printed and bound in the United States of America.

Library of Congress Cataloging-in-Publication Data is available.

To my parents, Carmen and Michele DeArdo,
and my siblings, Bryan DeArdo and Melanie McDonald.
God's first gift to me was you.

Joy depends on the cross.

—Thomas Merton, *The Sign of Jonas*

CONTENTS

FOREWORD

I am going to die.

You might remember the first time this thought stung your mind. Perhaps, like most people, you pushed away the thought and drowned it in busyness and pleasure. Most people spend at least part of their lives, if not all, fleeing from the uncomfortable reality of death rather than facing it head-on. But there are some exceptions. When Jesus' death drew near, "he set his face to go to Jerusalem" (Lk 9:51). Many of the early Christian martyrs went singing to their deaths. Bl. James Alberione, the founder of my religious order, the Daughters of St. Paul, kept a skull on his desk as a *memento mori*, or a reminder of death.

Several years back I decided to begin regularly meditating on my death. Like Bl. James Alberione, I acquired a small ceramic skull for my desk to remind myself that I will inevitably die. As I began this practice, I had no idea how much it would change my own life and the lives of others. I shared my memento mori journey on social media and, much to my surprise, thousands of people began to follow my posts with interest and to buy skulls for their own desks.

What must have seemed like a strange new fad to some was actually a revival of what used to be a widespread practice in the Church. *Memento mori*, Latin for "remember your death," has long been associated with the practice of reflecting on the unpredictable end of life. The spiritual practice of memento mori along with associated symbols and sayings were particularly popular in the medieval Church. But the tradition of contemplating one's mortality in order to live well is deeply rooted in salvation history.

St. Paul tells us, "sin came into the world through one man, and death came through sin" (Rom 5:12). For this reason, after the first sin God explicitly warns Adam to keep in mind his inevitable death: "You are dust, and to dust you shall return" (Gn 3:19). God's warning is the first of many such reminders in scripture. For example, the psalmist prays, "Teach us to count our days, that we may gain a wise heart" (Ps 90:12). And the book of Sirach urges, "In all you do, remember the end of your life, and then you will never sin" (7:36).

In the New Testament, Jesus exhorts his disciples, "If any want to become my followers, let them deny themselves and take up their cross daily and follow me" (Lk 9:23). I see this passage as another exhortation to the practice of regular meditation on death. After all, what does a person who is carrying his or her cross think of when following Jesus to the Place of the Skull? Death. Perhaps that is what inspired St. Benedict to exhort his monks to "keep death daily" before their eyes (*Rule* 4.47).

Regular meditation on death is a practice that philosophers and spiritual teachers, both inside and outside the Christian tradition, have encouraged for centuries. However, remembrance of death is completely different for the Christian. For us, death is not an inescapable, grim fate to which we must resign ourselves. Jesus conquered death and opened the gates of heaven through his death on the Cross. Astonishingly, for the Christian "dying is gain" (Phil 1:21). But do we really believe this? Can we really believe that death is gain without meditating on how the Cross has completely altered the trajectory of our lives in a personal, concrete way? Can we accept salvation without taking up our own crosses and accepting the sufferings and "little deaths" in our lives as we make our own way to heaven?

For most of us, the intentional, regular practice of memento mori is necessary to understand what Jesus has done for us and to avoid fleeing death and suffering in our lives. For others, memento mori is a way of life. The latter is true for Emily DeArdo. Since childhood, death has been her constant companion. At an age when most of us were catching butterflies and playing chase with our friends, she was diagnosed with life-threatening cystic fibrosis and was in and out of hospitals. Emily faced the inevitability of death earlier than most and, along with a great deal of suffering, it has accompanied her throughout her childhood and youth. But someone else also has accompanied her—Jesus.

In *Living Memento Mori*, Emily imparts the valuable lessons she has learned while suffering with Jesus by her side. Like the precious drops of Jesus' blood that spattered the Via Dolorosa, Emily shares valuable jewels of wisdom gleaned from a life lived in the shadow of death, a memento mori that has brought her closer to our Savior. As she will show, each of Jesus' steps on his way to the Place of the Skull reveals something to us. Our Savior Jesus Christ walked the Way of the Cross out of love for us, and he can teach us how to find peace and happiness by following in his footsteps.

As we walk alongside Jesus in this life, may he prepare us for a death that will lead to everlasting life.

Memento mori,
Sr. Theresa Aletheia Noble, F.S.P.

PREFACE

I was born at 2:47 p.m. on Good Friday. If my parents had been into omens, they might have taken note of this and been worried about my future. Being born on a day that's known for death is a bit grim, isn't it? This couldn't be a good thing, especially since I was a nice shade of Smurf blue and had an Apgar score of two.

Fortunately, it wasn't long before I turned a normal color; my mom got to hold me, and everything seemed to be OK. I was a fine, healthy baby.

Wasn't I?

Well . . . no. Not at all. We didn't know it then, but my tiny body was already waging war against itself. I had cystic fibrosis (CF), a fatal genetic disease that wouldn't be diagnosed until I was eleven years old.

Nemesis

When my pediatrician first mentioned "cystic fibrosis," I defaulted to my general coping mechanism: head to the books. On the creamy pages of our family's *World Book Encyclopedia*, I learned more about what I was facing. CF damages the lungs, pancreas, and other organs by affecting the way the body maintains the proper balance of salt and water. As the disease progresses, the organs become so scarred that they are unable to function. The book dispassionately stated that CF was fatal and that the average life span was thirty-three. At eleven, I thought that was a long way away. Thirty-three was *old*.

But even if I couldn't really verbalize it, I knew instantly that CF was going to kill me. And it tried really hard to do so. I contracted noninfectious tuberculosis when I was sixteen, and at nineteen, I spent two weeks in a medically induced coma, fighting off a bug that only one other person in the world had contracted. Nine months after I graduated from college, I was put on the donor list for a double-lung transplant. I weighed eighty-five pounds, and 19 percent of my lungs worked. I couldn't walk across a room without my heart jackhammering in my chest and my shoulders heaving. I knew that if a donor didn't come soon, I'd be dead by Christmas. Thankfully, a donor did come in time, and I've lived fourteen extra years of life with someone else's lungs inside me. However, that doesn't mean that my life is perfect now. As a result of the many medications I was on, both before and after the transplant, I've suffered profound hearing loss. In fact, three years after the transplant, I had a cochlear implant surgically placed in my head to give me back some of the hearing I had lost.

Still, living precariously balanced on the border between life and death made me think a lot about suffering, God, and what life's really all about. Maybe I never noticed it until after the transplant, but suddenly a rather strange truth was vividly alive for me—my life was sweeter, my prayer life deeper, and my relationship with God more personal because of what I've gone through. Facing death has taught me a lot about life. And I am grateful.

INTRODUCTION

Since *Living Memento Mori* is written around two main spiritual practices—memento mori and the Stations of the Cross—I thought it would be useful to give you a brief sketch of both—and some thoughts—before you dive in.

What Is Memento Mori?

Memento mori is a Latin phrase that means "remember that you will die" or "remember death." As a seashell memento reminds you of your vacation at the beach or your grandmother's brooch reminds you of your grandmother, so memento mori is an item that reminds you of your mortality, such as a skull on your desk or a picture of one as your laptop wallpaper.

Christians trace memento mori all the way back to the book of Genesis. There, after man and woman fell from grace, God lays out the consequences of sin and reminds them that they will die. "By the sweat of your face you shall eat bread," he says, "until you return to the ground, for out of it you were taken; you are dust, and to dust you shall return" (Gn 3:19).

The practice was also present in the pagan cultures of the ancient world. The Greek philosopher Socrates wrote, "The one aim of those who practice philosophy in the proper manner is to practice for dying and death." In Rome, generals who had won great battles were triumphantly paraded through the streets on chariots, hailed as divine beings. But at the elbow of the victorious general was a slave who whispered in the general's ear, "Respice post te. Hominem te esse memento. Memento mori!" That is, "Look behind. Remember you are human. Remember you will die!"

Queen Victoria wore a memento mori ring. St. Mary Magdalene and St. Jerome are often portrayed in art with a skull nearby, reminding them of their eventual demise and driving them to practice penance.

Morbid? Well, maybe. But at the same time, it's important that we remember we *will* die. It's going to happen someday. It could happen right after you finish reading this introduction. By living with a mindset of memento mori, we practice detachment from the things of this world and remind ourselves to live in a way that reflects our eternal destiny and inheritance. If we want to live with God forever in heaven, then we have to prepare for it as we're living here and now.

This is insanely countercultural, in a time when books with titles such as *How Not to Die* are found in bookstores and the culture seems obsessed with youth and eternal life on earth. John Lennon asked us to imagine that heaven doesn't exist. Catholics have a different worldview: not only do we have to *imagine* heaven but also we're called to live as if we want to go there!

Recently, there's been a resurgence of interest among Catholics in the practice of memento mori, and I'm heartened by this. Our spiritual lives can be enriched by remembering that, no matter how many vitamins we take or how many laps we swim, our bodies will eventually betray us. Embracing that reality can help us live in a way that is both fuller and more intentional; as Psalm 90 states, "Teach us to count our days, that we may gain a wise heart"(v. 12). By accepting that our days are limited, we can more clearly discern how to use the time we have on earth *well*.

You don't have to have a skull on your desk to remind you of death or hang a little skull on your keychain (although that might be a good conversation starter!). My memento mori is the large skin graft on my right arm that reminds me of the ways I've escaped death so far and that death will eventually come for me. It reminds me of what I've endured and that this life isn't all there is. In each chapter, we'll connect to the idea of memento mori.

The Stations of the Cross

Along with memento mori, each chapter of this book is focused on one of the fifteen Stations of the Cross. Also called the *Via Crucis* or the "Way of the Cross," the Stations of the Cross are designed to help people enter into Jesus' Passion and death more intensely. Prayer can take us there. By meditating on fourteen "stations," or moments, along Jesus' journey from his condemnation to his death and burial, we can be with Jesus as he walks the road to Calvary. Sometimes a fifteenth station, the Resurrection, is included—but not always.

The stations make up the spine of this book, and through them, I will share my own journey with you.

They are as follows:

1. Jesus is condemned to death.
2. Jesus takes up his Cross.
3. Jesus falls the first time.
4. Jesus meets his mother.
5. Simon helps Jesus carry his Cross.
6. Veronica wipes the face of Jesus.
7. Jesus falls the second time.
8. Jesus meets the women of Jerusalem.
9. Jesus falls the third time.
10. Jesus is stripped of his garments.
11. Jesus is nailed to the Cross.
12. Jesus dies.

13. Jesus is taken down from the Cross.
14. Jesus is buried.
15. Jesus rises from the dead.

It is particularly popular to pray the Stations of the Cross during Lent, but they can be prayed at any time. Most Catholic churches have the stations erected along the walls, so you can pray before each one and move along as they progress, thereby making a miniature Way of the Cross, allowing you to walk with Jesus through his Passion and death.

The Cross Is the Key

In my Catholic elementary school, crucifixes were everywhere, from the cafeteria to the library to the gym. My classmates and I spent our days looking at the crucifix hung above the blackboard as a constant reminder of what Jesus had done for us.

The crucifixes weren't there because we Catholics are obsessively focused on pain and death. The crucifixes were there because our faith teaches us that the Cross of Christ isn't just a *thing*, some holy decoration; it's a *way* that leads us to something more, not only in eternity but also right here on earth. One of my favorite saints, St. Elizabeth Ann Seton, said, "Can you expect to go to heaven for nothing? Did not our Savior track the whole way to it with his tears and blood?" We can't expect otherwise. We are going to suffer. We are going to experience pain. And, yes, we are going to die.

The crucifix can be seen in two ways: as a gory, unnecessary reminder of Christ's suffering for our sins *or* as the Tree of Life. In everything we experience in life—suffering and joy, pain and happiness, doubt and certainty—Jesus understands us. He became one of us, and he gives us an example of how to live, especially in the face of suffering. "For to this you have been called, because Christ also suffered for you, leaving you an example, so that you should follow in his steps," St. Peter tells us (1 Pt 2:21).

But do we really *believe* this? Do we believe that Jesus understands our emotions, our pain and suffering, and helps us carry it? Do we believe there's some *point* to all of this?

I do. And I want you to as well. Practicing memento mori has enriched my life in profound ways. As we go along, I'll share with you my experiences of how these reflections have led me to a deeper trust in God and a closer relationship with him. I'll also draw from Pope John Paul II's 1984 apostolic letter *On the Christian Meaning of Human Suffering* (*Salvifici Doloris*). The wisdom of John Paul II has comforted me; his words have also challenged me to learn how to join my suffering to the Passion of Christ.

Headed to Heaven

As Catholic Christians, we believe in the resurrection of the dead. Heaven, we trust, is a place of eternal happiness because we're with God, and *nothing* is better than that. Heaven is indescribably beautiful and perfect. St. Paul wrote that "no eye has seen, nor ear heard, nor the heart of man conceived, what God has prepared for those who love him" (1 Cor 2:9).

We should all, then, long for heaven. Of course, the problem is that to get there, we have to die. And that's where most of us get off the train. *I was with you until you brought up the death thing, Emily . . . but now I'd like to go back to my blissful, Instagram-perfect life with flowers and butterflies, please.*

Holding on to what our faith teaches us about suffering and death is made harder by the fact that these are not welcome ideas in twenty-first-century America. As a culture, we don't want to see disability, hear about suffering, or face death. We run in the opposite direction. Our society hides pain behind the walls of hospitals and assisted living homes and wraps it in sterile bandages and impersonal medical charts. This is not a Christian way to view life—or live it. Deep in our hearts, we know that suffering and death cannot be avoided, and yet we run from it, as does Voldemort in the Harry Potter novels. It didn't work for him, and it won't work for us.

Take Up Your Cross

When Jesus tells us to take up our cross and follow him, he means it. None of us will have a life without adversity or hardship; we are all dying. But because Jesus, the beloved Son of the Father, suffered and died, we always have someone to turn to, someone who can teach us how to suffer in a way that leads to redemption. We can also turn to one another. Living with cystic fibrosis has shown me that suffering doesn't mean that life is doomed to be dark and terrible. Every human life, even with suffering and often *because* of it, can lead to joy and deeper intimacy with God.

Death may loom large in your mind or be something you find difficult to imagine. Your cross may not be a physical illness, like mine is. It may be emotional, financial, mental, job or family related, or a combination of all of these. The weight of it might be new to you or an old familiar nemesis. But whatever it is, Jesus knows it. And Jesus is there to help you carry it, all the way home.

CHAPTER 1
THE END IN SIGHT

If we live, we live to the Lord, and if we die, we die to the Lord; so then, whether we live or whether we die, we are the Lord's.

—Romans 14:8

Jesus knew it would come to this. His life had been moving toward this moment: this stone pavement in Jerusalem and a Roman governor condemning him to death before a baying crowd—a crowd of people that he loved.

In his book *Death on a Friday Afternoon*, Fr. Richard John Neuhaus writes that "the way of the cross is the way of broken hearts."[1] His body was broken and bleeding, but I suspect Jesus felt his heart break too. To experience the lack of love and understanding, the absence of mercy in the faces and voices of those calling out "Crucify him!" must have been as painful as the scourging whips.

Here the Lord of Life faced death. Jesus is wholly God, but he is also wholly human. And no human being desires pain or celebrates when death is imminent.

The Shadow of Death

How old were you when you first encountered death? The first I remember was the death of our pastor when I was eleven years old. Monsignor Donovan was a gentle man with a soft Irish brogue. He began all his homilies with "my dear brothers and sisters in Christ" and ended them with "and may God bless you." He died of a heart attack, and I cried myself to sleep the night we got the news. Now, all of a sudden, the priest who kept two lambs on the rectory grounds and who perpetually smiled was gone. That was what really shook me about death—the finality of it.

We walk through the valley of the shadow of death every day (see Psalm 23), but it's easy to forget about it. Until we get a phone call. Or an email. Or your doctor says, "I want more tests done." Or your spouse says, "I don't love you anymore." Or a child slams the door and walks out of your house and seemingly out of your life. Dreams punctured by the sting of rejection, friendships that decay, and relatives you don't speak to, even though you can't remember why, are all part of death. Death casts long shadows, and broken hearts come in many varieties.

"Come and Die"

Christian thought has long connected the idea of suffering and spiritual growth. Dietrich Bonhoeffer, a German pastor and theologian who resisted the Nazi regime, wrote, "When Christ calls a man, he bids him come and die."[2] C. S. Lewis, a British professor and lay theologian, wrote, "If you think of this world as a place intended simply for our happiness, you find it quite intolerable; think of it as a place of training and correction and it's not so bad."[3]

And that's part of the problem, isn't it? We don't *want* to come and die. We don't *want* correction. We don't *want* to suffer, and that makes complete sense, because we're hardwired to avoid pain.

But pain is also what wakes us up. Once the marriage dissolves, the phone call comes, or the friendship ends—that is, when we're in a position of brokenheartedness—we are much more amenable (at least in my experience) to reach out to God. The few times we talk to God when things are going well are too often with a sort of perfunctory, "Oh, thank God everything is happening the way I want it!" But God wants more from us than just our thanks when things are the way we want them to be. He wants our whole hearts and our whole lives. Suffering is going to come but, with it, an opportunity to grow closer to God.

Suffering with Purpose

During his pontificate, Pope John Paul II wrote his apostolic letter *On the Christian Meaning of Human Suffering* (*Salvifici Doloris*), which grapples with the idea of human suffering and how we as Christians, who believe in a loving God, can respond to it. I have found his words both comforting and challenging. In the beginning of the letter, the pope writes that "'suffering' seems to be particularly *essential to the nature of man. . . .* It can be said that man in a special fashion becomes the way for the Church when suffering enters his life. . . . In whatever form, suffering seems to be, and is, almost *inseparable from man's earthly existence*" (SD 2, 3).

This isn't anything new. Everyone knows we suffer, everyone knows we die, and everyone knows life isn't fair. Thanks, Pope John Paul II, for pointing out the obvious! We suffer, and Jesus suffered. But how does that connect to us, today, in our very real suffering? The pope gives us an answer: "Every man has *his own share in the Redemption. . . .* In bringing about the Redemption through suffering, Christ *has* also *raised human suffering to the level of the Redemption.* Thus each man, in his suffering, can also become a sharer in the redemptive suffering of Christ" (SD 19).

St. Paul also wrote about this shared suffering in his letter to the Philippians: "For his sake, I have suffered the loss of all things, and I regard them as rubbish, in order that I may gain Christ" (Phil 3:8). St. Paul knew what we all need to learn—that suffering is completely inseparable from being a Christian. You aren't going to find a prosperity gospel preached here. Yet our suffering can be more than just our personal pain: we don't have to lose ourselves in one big pity party. Instead, we can join our sorrows to the sufferings of Christ.

That doesn't mean, however, that Christians are, or should become, masochists. We're not actively *looking* for martyrdom or suffering. That's not good either. Yes, we're called to practice penance, but that doesn't mean we go looking for ways to make our lives harder just so we can suffer and get some sort of heavenly brownie points. We are called to accept what's given to us by God.

The more we are able to accept unavoidable suffering throughout our lives, the more comfortable we become with it, and the more comfortable we become with death. When we experience loss, pain, and suffering, we have an opportunity to practice acceptance by letting go of our desires and plans and submitting our will to the will of God. Death is the final surrender to God. By accepting God's will, we are rehearsing for that final acceptance—the day God calls us home.

Death Sentence

When I was diagnosed with cystic fibrosis (CF), I didn't consciously join my sufferings to Christ's. I wasn't some pint-sized saint. (I'm still not—pint-sized or a saint!) I didn't rejoice, but I didn't cry either. I just went along with what my parents and doctors and nurses told me to do. And after spending two weeks in the hospital for IV medications, education, and a battery of tests, I went back to school.

Outwardly, nothing was different. I still played clarinet in the band, still hated math class, and still loved to sing and read. But now I went to the nurse's office before lunch to get two enzymes from the bottle with my name on it that sat in her med drawer. Now I got early dismissals from school every three months to see my pulmonologist.

I knew from reading the encyclopedia that CF was fatal. I had been given my death sentence as surely as Jesus had been given his on the stone pavement that day in Jerusalem. But *life went on*. In the span of thirty-six hours, I'd been diagnosed with a fatal disease and was sitting in a strange hospital room, being poked with needles and facing an army of new terms, procedures, and vocabulary. *My* world had completely changed—but *the* world didn't seem to notice.

As If Nothing Happened

That's how it generally goes, isn't it? You get news that shatters your world to its core and smashes your heart into a million pieces. And yet you still have to do laundry and make dinner and put gas in the car. It was the same for Jesus. On that day in Jerusalem, people still had to earn a living, clean their homes for Passover, buy vegetables or fruits for dinner, get water at the well, tell their kids to stop fighting, and set the table.

But even if the world doesn't stop, Jesus does. He knows what we're going through when our hearts break. Jesus knows what it feels like to be judged, to lose everything, and to receive a death sentence. Let's not write that off too lightly. Let's not forget how intimately Jesus knows us and our human nature. As the letter to the Hebrews says, "For we do not have a high priest who is unable to sympathize with our weaknesses, but we have one who in every respect has been tested as we are, yet without sin. Let us therefore approach the throne of grace with boldness, so that we may receive mercy and find grace to help in time of need" (Heb 4:15–16). In our heartbreak, we can go to the Lord, and he *wants* us to come to him. The question isn't whether Jesus is with us; the question is whether we will turn toward him or away from him in our pain.

When we find ourselves standing on our own stone pavements, and our lives are irrevocably changed, Jesus is standing there with us.

And when we find ourselves face-to-face with judgment and death or at the beginning of a difficult path we did not choose, the Son of God holds out his hand and says, "Let's begin the journey."

Will you?

Questions along the Way of Your Cross

1. When was the first time you experienced death? How old were you? Journal about that experience and how it's shaped the way you look at and experience death or loss.
2. Have you ever thought about your own death? Why or why not? What scares about death?
3. Have you accepted Jesus' invitation to walk with him in times of suffering? If so, how? If not, how might you do that today?

CHAPTER 2
THE THINGS WE CARRY

> If any want to become my followers, let them deny
> themselves and take up their cross and follow me. For
> those who want to save their life will lose it, and those
> who lose their life for my sake, and for the sake of the
> gospel, will save it.
>
> —Mark 8:34–35

What Jesus tells his disciples here is shocking. Today, the phrase "take up your cross" has all the punch of a Catholic grandmother saying, "Offer it up for the souls in purgatory!" It's become so familiar that we don't really hear it anymore. But when Jesus spoke these words to his original audience, it was the equivalent of telling a twenty-first-century crowd to pull up an electric chair and sit down. Who wants to do that? Subject yourself to an instrument of death (and not just death but painful, agonizing, humiliating death) to follow this guy? No thanks.

Jesus' words, however, always match his actions. He never asks us to do something that he isn't willing to do himself. With his first steps toward Calvary, Jesus not only takes up his cross but does so willingly. This willingness is depicted beautifully in the 2004 film *The Passion of the Christ*. There, Jesus embraces his Cross—falling down in front of it and wrapping his arms around it while one of the thieves rails at him, calling him a fool. But Jesus knew something the thief didn't, something we often lose sight of—that his Cross is the Tree of Life. Remember what Jesus told his apostles: he had come to lay down his life for the sheep—for us. "For this reason the

Father loves me, because I lay down my life in order to take it again" (Jn 10:17). Jesus will see out that charge until his very last breath.

Do Not Be Afraid

Well, that's all good and well for Jesus, you might object. *He knew how the story was going to end. I have no idea how my story will end. I just know that death and suffering are going to come, and I'm not sure I can carry that.*

That's a logical objection. Who would blindly follow someone into death and pain and torture? No one, right? But that's what happened when we were baptized. We are, after all, baptized into the death of Christ so that we can rise with him. It's also what happens when we decide to take our Christian faith personally. We choose to follow Jesus anywhere he leads us, and often, he leads us right to the Cross. But at the same time, Jesus also tells us not to be afraid, not to let our hearts be troubled (see John 14:27).

In short—we're supposed to trust him. Deeply. Every step of the way. While we're struggling to carry our crosses. And of course, we don't know the way. But then again, neither did the disciples. Thomas asked Jesus that at the Last Supper: "Lord, we do not know where you are going. How can we know the way?" (Jn 14:5). But we have an advantage over Thomas. We know that the end of every Christian story is eternal life with Jesus (we hope). Heaven, after all, is our goal. But to get to heaven, we have to die, and because we have to die, we ought to think about death.

Nonnegotiable

If we want heaven, then the Cross is nonnegotiable and so is the Way of the Cross. If we want the fullest life, life forever with Christ, then we have to set our sights there and prepare for it. Athletes know this. If you want to be in the Olympics, you can't just dream about it, read

Runner's World magazine, and plod around the neighborhood a few times a week. Your entire life has to revolve around reaching your goal—how you sleep, how you eat, how you train, and even how you rest. As Christians, we're called to do no less. I can't think of a single saint who got to heaven just by thinking nice thoughts and going to Mass once a week. It doesn't work that way. As St. Rose of Lima said, "Apart from the cross, there is no other way to get to heaven."

So, yes, we have to think about death. We have to keep our goal in sight, and that means we have to stop turning away from the instruments of death to self and sin in our lives and start learning how to embrace them. Follow St. Paul's admonishment: "Do you not know that in a race all the runners compete, but only one receives the prize? Run in such a way that you may win it. Athletes exercise self-control in all things; they do it to receive a perishable wreath, *but we an imperishable one*" (1 Cor 9:24–25; emphasis added).

Suffering for Good

Yet learning to acknowledge the reality of death will not be easy. Crosses aren't meant to be easy. We will struggle with them. We will fall under the weight of them. They will dig into our shoulders, and carrying them will hurt. In other words, we will suffer. Why? John Paul II has an answer. "It can be said that man suffers whenever *he experiences any kind of evil.* . . . We could say that man suffers *because of a good* in which he does not share. . . . He particularly suffers when he 'ought'—in the normal order of things—to have a share in this good and does not have it" (SD 7).

Single people who want to get married feel the lack of a spouse because marriage is a good thing. People who are sick suffer for lack of health. Divorced people suffer the lack of a loving marriage. Couples who long to have a child but struggle with infertility suffer because having children is a good thing. Suffering is not an evil *in itself*, but it *is* the result of some sort of evil in our lives, whether it's biological evil (a disease), emotional evil (betrayal or the failure of a relationship), or some other sort.

Whether visible or invisible, everyone has a cross. In my life I've suffered many misunderstandings or assumptions from other people because I looked healthy. People didn't understand why I had a handicapped placard for my car when I appeared perfectly able-bodied. These days, people don't understand why I don't answer their questions because they can't see the cochlear implant that's tucked under my hair. They don't know that I'm hearing impaired, so misunderstandings arise. All of these are part of my cross, and everyone's cross is multifaceted. It's usually not just *one* thing that hurts as we drag our crosses through our lives. It's multiple things.

No One to Blame

It's important to remember, too, that suffering is hardly ever caused by something we did. Certainly, our choices have consequences and our actions can cause suffering. But a cross is not some cosmic punishment from God. "*It is not true* that *all suffering is a consequence of a fault and has a nature of a punishment*," John Paul II writes (SD 11). And Jesus says the same thing in the Gospel of John: "As he walked along, he saw a man blind from birth. His disciples asked him, 'Rabbi, who sinned, this man or his parents, that he was born blind?' Jesus answered, 'Neither this man nor his parents sinned; he was born blind so that God's works might be revealed in him'" (Jn 9:1–3).

Again, the cross is *not* a punishment from God, although it can seem that way, because the cross is an instrument of death. There's no happy connotation to a cross—*unless* we look at it as the instrument of our salvation, as the Tree of Life.

Our crosses can be united to his Cross. We don't have to carry the cross alone. But neither can we just look at our cross and refuse to carry it. Jesus didn't say, "*Look at* your cross and follow me." He said, "*Take up* your cross."

How do we do that, when the cross is so intimidating? Jesus' Cross probably weighed between seventy and one hundred pounds. That's a significant weight for most people, but for Jesus, who had been scourged and was dehydrated and hungry, it was even worse. Picking up his Cross was a monumental task.

In my own life, I've found that sometimes I have to rant and rave about the particular cross awhile before I'm ready to pick it up. When my doctors wanted to put a port-a-cath under my skin to give me almost instant IV access because my veins were shot, I rebelled a bit. When the idea of a cochlear implant was first presented to me, I hated the idea. Sometimes we have to yell and get it out of our system.

But then we can choose to look at the cross, breathe deeply, and pick it up. Even if we grunt and groan and feel as if it will crush us, we can try to pick it up. Jesus says that his yoke is easy and his burden light. Believe him. Try to lift the burden. You might not be able to do it all at one time. You might have to adjust yourself to the weight of one piece and then try to shoulder more. It might be a gradual process, and that's OK. The point is that you try to accept these sufferings because, as with Jesus' Cross, they ultimately lead us to life.

Questions along the Way of Your Cross

1. Is there a cross in your life that you are avoiding and have not yet embraced?
2. Do you struggle with the idea that the suffering in your life is God's punishment?

3.   What is your life's goal? What are you willing to do to reach it?

CHAPTER 3
FALLING IN LOVE

But he was wounded for our transgressions,
   crushed for our iniquities;
upon him was the punishment that made us whole,
   and by his bruises we are healed.

—Isaiah 53:5

The route from Jerusalem to Golgotha was about half a mile. It passed through narrow lanes, was mostly uphill, and led out of the city to a hilltop where executions took place. *Golgotha*, in Jesus' native Aramaic, meant "skull."

Jesus hasn't had anything to eat since the Last Supper on Holy Thursday night. It's early Friday morning. Maybe he's had some water in his prison cell the night before, but if he did, it wasn't much. He's been beaten and scourged; a crown of thorns has been pressed onto his head; he has been mocked and spit upon. And now the crowd presses in on all sides. Because humiliation was also part of the punishment, people watched the procession and jeered at the criminals as they passed by.

Most of us have probably had to run a mile in gym class. If you're a nonrunner like me, it's not the most fun thing you've ever done. Still, I'd had a good night's sleep, breakfast, and access to plenty of water to drink as I ran. I could stop if I needed to. I turned on my Walkman and ran to *The Phantom of the Opera*. It wasn't fun, but it wasn't torture.

Jesus' route was torturous. But unlike me, Jesus had a supreme goal in mind: the salvation of our bodies and souls. His was motivated by love. Every slow, tortured step, with the massive weight of the Cross bearing down on him, brought him not only closer to death but also closer to fulfilling his purpose.

He wasn't walking to get a gym credit. He was walking, struggling, and falling because he loved us.

Loved to Death

Think of the person you love the most. It might be your spouse, your kids (or both), your parents, siblings, or best friend—whoever it is, think about them.

Now: How far does your love for them go? Would you be willing to die for them?

Really—think about it honestly. Don't just give a knee-jerk, "Yeah, sure, OK." Really think about this. Would you *die* to save their lives? Not just be inconvenienced, not just sort of suffer—*die*. For your family members, you'd probably say yes, especially if it's your spouse or your children.

I have a lot of great friends. I'd give them a kidney, blood, or money. I'd *suffer* for them. I'd inconvenience myself for them. But (no offense, friends reading this) I'm not sure I'd be willing to die for them. And these are people I really love.

Our human love pales in comparison to Jesus' love for us. I say "love" when I talk about books, *The Wizard of Oz*, Chuy's creamy jalapeño dip, or hockey. We "love" ice cream and chocolate and our car, or the beach. In our lexicon, it's a word that's stronger than "like." For Jesus, love means total self-giving. It means love to the point of death.

That's the motivation behind everything he does. It's not because he wants to make us suffer, make our lives harder, or give us a set of rules to live by (although there are some rules). His motivation is love. Real, entire, self-giving, self-sacrificing love. Love that leads to death—and then to life again.

His love isn't selfish. It's not self-interested or self-motivated. It's everything that St. Paul talks about in 1 Corinthians 13 (aka the reading we've all heard at every wedding since forever). His love is real, just as his suffering is, and it drives him to death for our sakes.

"Human suffering," John Paul II writes, "has reached its culmination in the Passion of Christ. And at the same time it has entered into a completely new dimension and a new order: *it has been linked to love*, to means of suffering, just as the supreme good of the Redemption of the world was drawn from the Cross of Christ" (SD 18).

Jesus didn't love death. He loved us to the point of death. Is your love like that?

Falling Under the Weight

How does this love play out in your personal way of the cross? There are times, I'm sure, when it doesn't feel like love. It feels like punishment.

You might have accepted your cross. You've gotten over the heartbreak of the initial experience. You've started to live life under the new burden that you're carrying—the job loss, the divorce, the wayward sibling, or the chemo treatments. You think you have a plan.

But then something else happens, and it all falls to pieces. *You* fall to pieces.

By the time I was fifteen, I'd been living the CF life for four years. We thought we knew the ropes. When I started to feel more fatigued, when my coughing increased, and when my appetite decreased, the doctors said "that was just how CF went."

But I sensed something else was wrong.

And something *was* wrong. My favorite doctor, Dr. McCoy, decided to dig deeper and ordered various tests and procedures that led to the bizarre diagnosis of noninfectious tuberculosis. About 4 percent of the CF population gets this particular bug. It came out of left field—seriously, who gets tuberculosis in a first-world country these days?

Me. That's who. I do.

Fortunately, it was treatable with oral meds. Unfortunately, though, these medicines were really hard on my body. They made my stomach hurt so much that I didn't want to eat anything. I actually cried at the thought of having to eat a bowl of ice cream (who does that?!). And I had to take these meds for three years.

Eventually, my body adjusted, and I kicked the nasty bug to the curb. But the initial few months were rough. I was barely staying awake in school. I stopped my private voice lessons because I just couldn't handle that work on top of trying to stay awake in my classes. I was a *mess*.

I didn't feel as if God had abandoned me because I knew he hadn't. Still, I wasn't really *pleased* with this turn of events. If Dr. McCoy hadn't thought to do more testing, I'd have died—at sixteen. So yes, I was suffering a setback, a fall.

The Light of Salvation

John Paul II shares a pertinent thought: "And even though the victory over sin and death achieved by Christ in his Cross and Resurrection does not abolish temporal suffering from human life . . . it nevertheless *throws a new light* upon this dimension and upon every suffering: the light of salvation" (SD 15).

God doesn't take away our suffering, no matter how much we might wish he would. Every human life will have it. But there is comfort—at least to me—in the truth that we are not alone and that it guides us to salvation.

We fall as Christ falls under the weight of the cross. We might feel this is unfair because, we could argue, Jesus *voluntarily* chose this route, and we did not. But that doesn't mean his choice was *easy* or that it was pain-free.

The Struggle Is Real

All suffering is real, both Jesus' and ours. But the purpose hidden in suffering is just as real. In the middle of the dusty road, crushed by your cross's weight, you might not see that. Instead, you might be tempted to stay right where you fell or get up only to throw the cross away and run away screaming from God's idea of "love." (As St. Teresa of Avila said, "God, if this is how you treat your friends, no wonder you have so few!") It's the same when we think about death: we want to run away from the idea, from the fear of the unknown. We don't want to think about it, and we certainly don't want to embrace it. Death is terrifying.

In our falls, in the times when we let go or lose our grip on our crosses and face anew the horror of our suffering, we are not alone. Jesus, too, looked into the darkness of death and experienced pain. He knows and understands how we feel better than anyone else could. Love led him to this. Is love leading you?

Let your love extend to loving Jesus enough to trust him. Trust him enough to get back up and continue to walk with him. Don't let fear and pain deter you.

Questions along the Way of Your Cross

1. Can you see the parallels between the suffering of Jesus and the suffering in your life? What purpose can your falls serve?

2. When have you felt wounded and bruised? How did that situation turn out in your life? If you're still in that situation, have you been able to entrust it to God?

3. Do you believe that Christ understands your sufferings? Or does he seem too remote and distant?

CHAPTER 4
IN IT TOGETHER

Then Simeon blessed them and said to his mother Mary,
"This child is destined for the falling and the rising of
many in Israel, and to be a sign that will be opposed so
that the inner thoughts of many will be revealed—and
a sword will pierce your own soul too."

—Luke 2:34–35

If the Way of the Cross is the way of broken hearts, then Mary's heart
was probably disintegrating on Good Friday. Her son, her baby,
her only child was being put to death. Was she remembering what
Simeon had said to her all those years ago? Was this the sword he had
prophesized? It must have felt like a dozen swords piercing her heart.

No mother wants to watch her child suffer. But Mary didn't
hide from her son's suffering. She witnessed it, and even more than
that—she *accompanied* him in it. This was all she could do for him
now. This time, she couldn't tell Jesus that it was going to be all
right. She couldn't hug him or kiss away his tears. This time, she
was powerless to do anything to stop what was happening. But she
also trusted God with *why* it was happening.

The Cross of Witness

One of the things that, I think, plays into our fear of death and
suffering is the idea that we will be helpless, that we won't be able
to do things for ourselves. We will lose our agency. And this sense
of powerlessness certainly applies to watching people we love suffer.

Can you watch your sibling, your baby, or your parent suffer without wanting to help, even if it's just listening to them pour out their sorrows? I've seen my father become livid with hospital workers who weren't working fast enough (in his opinion) to help me. Once I apologized to a nurse about it later. She said, "It's just because he loves you." And it's true. Love drives us to want to do *something*.

But sometimes we can't do *anything* to help. There was nothing Mary could do to help her son, except to be present. Mary didn't run away. She could have. She could've said, "I can't handle this," and stayed home. But she didn't. Her choice here is powerful.

Mary's choice could be called the cross of witness. We feel the futility of watching someone we love suffer, and this is heavy and painful. We want to stop the suffering of the person we love or stop death in its tracks—and we can't. Mary understands this.

Unshakable Faith

My parents have always had a special devotion to Mary, and I think it's helped them handle the times when they've had to watch me suffer. Yes, I was the one physically in pain, but seeing their daughter in an ICU bed, so still and *quiet* (I am never quiet), must have been terrifying. I was nine months old the first time I was admitted to the hospital. Watching their little girl, their only child, in a crib that looked more like a cage, with IV lines in tiny arms, must have been torturous. We didn't know at the time that the digestive problems I was having were indications of something much more serious.

And yet they knew what many Catholics know: that Mary "bears *by her whole life* . . . this particular Gospel of suffering" (SD 25). As John Paul II puts it, Mary's suffering reaches "an intensity which can hardly be imagined from a human point of view but which was mysterious and supernaturally fruitful for the redemption of the world" (SD 25).

Unceasing Help

My mom loves the image of Mary as Our Lady of Perpetual Help. If you're not familiar with this image, it's a fifteenth-century Byzantine icon that pictures Mary holding a toddler-age Jesus. The archangel Gabriel is on Mary's right, holding a three-bar cross, which was used by popes at the time, while the archangel Michael is on her left, holding the lance and the sponge that would be used at Jesus' crucifixion.

But the really interesting part of the icon is easily overlooked. One of Jesus' sandals is dangling off his foot. According to the icon's story, the toddler-aged Jesus had seen what was going to happen to him during his Passion and was so frightened that he ran to his mother for comfort.

When I asked my mom why this was her favorite image of Mary, she mentioned that last point: "Mary is trying to console Jesus, but she knows what's going to happen to him. His fear is so visceral; he's afraid and he's run to his mother for comfort. It was like when I tried to give you hope, even though I knew what was ahead of you."

Mary's humanity is something that even secular media grasps when they talk about Catholicism. In the television show *Outlander*, based on the best-selling book series by author Diana Gabaldon, Marian imagery is used in a poignant way. In the second season, Claire, the protagonist, suffers a miscarriage, losing her daughter, named Faith. While she's recovering in the hospital run by French sisters, one of the sisters puts a statue of Mary by Claire's bed, explaining her actions with "She lost a child too."

Mary knows sorrow and she knows loss. She knows pain and uncertainty, and above all, she knows what it's like to lose the person she loves most. First and foremost, Mary is a mother. Even those of us who aren't mothers know that comforting their children is part of a mother's vocation. We run to them when we're hurt, we cry on their shoulders, and we're held against their breasts as babies.

Because Jesus is God, his suffering can seem remote sometimes. But Mary's suffering is completely, achingly human. She's the sorrowful mother standing at the Cross, watching her only son suffocate and bleed—for us.

Mary understands our feelings of frustration and futility; she knows what it's like to look for hope in helplessness.

Questions along the Way of Your Cross

1. Do you find it harder to suffer or to watch someone you love suffer?
2. Do you relate to Mary more as the joyful young mother at Christmas or the sorrowful and seasoned mother at the Cross?
3. What makes you feel powerless? How do you respond to situations in which you can do little or nothing?

CHAPTER 5
A HELPING HAND

Bear one another's burdens, and in this way you will
fulfill the law of Christ.

—Galatians 6:2

As Jesus winds through the streets of Jerusalem with his Cross, things
start to change. He is surrounded by people, and some of them tease
and taunt him; they may even throw things at him. His strength
is waning as the heat of the day grows and the road continues to
climb. He's had the emotional encounter with his mother, which
might have given him strength, but it also might have depleted
him even more. At this point, Jesus is so physically weak that the
Romans begin to worry that he'll die before he makes it to Calvary.
They know that Jesus is struggling, and they pull someone from the
crowd to help him. St. Mark's gospel says that Simon of Cyrene is
"compelled" (Mk 15:21), that is, forced, into service.

We don't know much about Simon, other than he had two
children, Alexander and Rufus, and that he was "coming in from
the country" (Mk 15:21). Cyrene is a city in eastern Libya, and the
journey from there to Jerusalem is a long one. He had been traveling for quite some time. He was tired. He was probably hungry.
He came to Jerusalem from Africa for Passover. He definitely didn't
imagine that he'd be helping a condemned criminal carry his cross.
It was probably a repulsive idea. Simon was just going about his day
in an unfamiliar place, and suddenly he was shouldering a heavy
cross with some condemned criminal? This was not how he thought

this Friday was going to go. He was subjected to the jeers and the taunts as well as perhaps being hit by objects thrown by the crowd. The man he walks next to is battered, bloody, and beaten.

But clearly, something happened to Simon on that day because tradition says that his sons, Alexander and Rufus, were widely known missionaries in the early Church. This didn't turn out to be a one-and-done thing for Simon. He must have thought about Jesus all through his time in Jerusalem and on the long trip home. What he experienced made a big enough impression on him that he told his children about Jesus.

Chance encounters and unexpected demands can turn our lives upside down.

Vulnerability

Do you like being vulnerable? I can probably answer that for you—you don't. Not many people do. It means showing our most sensitive thoughts and feelings—our weaknesses—to people who might ridicule or reject us. It's scary to let people into our sufferings and to show them the real us, with all our flaws, foibles, and fears. And there is nothing that makes us more vulnerable than knowing we are going to die. No matter how many books we read or how many superfoods we eat, our earthly lives will end. Our bodies, which we spend so much time getting into shape, will decay. It's not a pretty thought, but it's a true one.

Realizing this vulnerability can help us to evaluate our lives more appropriately. Does it really *matter* if the cookies are perfect for the scout banquet—or it is more important that you let your son help you bake them? Can you let go of the desire to appear perfectly pulled together and let people into your life by sharing what's really going on behind the perfectly coiffed appearance? Can you stop faking that you're fine?

Life's too short to worry about whether your sadness and worry are successfully hidden. If you try to be too strong, the facade will eventually crack. No one can be strong alone forever.

Being vulnerable isn't always a bad thing. In fact, it can be life-saving.

Flights of Stairs

I never wanted anyone to feel "sorry" for me. I wanted everyone to see me as just as capable as everyone else. So I never asked for special privileges. I never told anyone if they were walking too fast for me or that I really shouldn't be sitting in smoking sections (this was when places still had smoking sections). I didn't want to cause trouble or need special accommodation. I wanted to be like everyone else. I didn't want to be difficult.

Keeping up this facade got harder as my CF advanced. As my lung function declined, I had to make my needs more clearly known. As much as I hated it, I didn't have a choice. I made my friends wait for a table in the nonsmoking section as opposed to taking the first available table. I couldn't walk as far as they could, so I asked for them to park in closer parking spaces. Sometimes people would complain, but usually my friends complied.

And sometimes they did more than comply. Sometimes they actually *carried* me.

A few college friends and I went to New York City for New Year's Eve in 2003. It was one of those typical college trips: you rent a big van, drive into the city, cram into a hotel room, and stay there for three days, doing the entire city as quickly as possible on a college student's budget. On the first night, everyone wanted to visit the Empire State Building.

Of course, it was crowded with New Year's tourists. There were elevators to take us to certain floors, but at the last stop before the top, my friends decided to climb the stairs to the observation deck instead of waiting in the long elevator lines.

I hesitated. I was pretty sure I wasn't going to be able to climb all those stairs. But I didn't want to lose my friends and get lost in the huge crowd of people. So I followed them.

After about two flights, I leaned against the concrete wall of the stairwell, panting, my heart hammering. I didn't think I'd make it to the top—and most of my friends had gone on ahead of me. Clusters of people passed me as I gasped for breath. I was pretty sure my face was a pasty white color and that I looked awful, but I didn't really care. I just wanted to breathe easily again, even if that meant sitting in this stairwell for the rest of the night.

But suddenly, I was being picked up and carried in someone's arms.

Without saying a word, my friend Chris, who had come back to check on me, decided to pick me up and carry me to the observation deck.

He didn't make a big deal about it. Part of me was embarrassed that I was twenty-one years old and needed to be carried, but part of me was really glad that I had a friend who would put himself out to help me like that. Sure, I didn't weigh a whole lot (I think I was about ninety-seven pounds at that point), but he saw the need, he saw my vulnerability, and he helped me. He didn't have to. But he did.

Good Samaritans

Chris was acting, on that frigid December night, as my Good Samaritan. John Paul II says that "we are not allowed to 'pass by on the other side' indifferently; we must 'stop' beside him. *Everyone who stops beside the suffering of another person*, whatever form it may take, is a Good Samaritan. This stopping does not mean curiosity but availability" (SD 28).

Availability is what my best friend Anne and her mom showed when they came to visit me the night I was first admitted to the hospital in 1993. They weren't being curious, like the rubberneckers on the highway around an accident. Anne was being *available*, and so was her mom. They were providing my parents and me with a much-needed island of familiarity, friendship, and comfort in that room on Five Tower. Anne brought me a boxed set of the *Misty of Chincoteague* books, because of our mutual love of horses. We talked about the books, my new Felicity doll, and our classes at school. She didn't ask about the IV in the crook of my arm. She didn't ask what CF was or what it meant for me. We just talked about the things we loved, as we always did.

Anne and her mother didn't have to visit me. Chris didn't have to carry me. But they were "*sensitive to the sufferings of others*" (SD 28). They came because I needed them. They might not put it this way, but they were giving me what John Paul II calls the "gift of self" (SD 28).

Letting Ourselves Be Helped

We all need Good Samaritans on our journeys. But we have to *let* ourselves be open to the help of the people that God puts in our path.

Simon *had* to help Jesus. He wasn't given a choice. But Jesus accepted his help. (After all, Jesus could have called down twelve legions of angels.) But he's teaching us a valuable lesson here: We need each other. We can't do things alone. And more, we *shouldn't* do things alone. The life of those who follow Jesus is one of love and service—and we will be on both ends in the course of our lives.

We ought to be willing to help, but we also need to learn to accept help gracefully.

As I got more and more sick, I was forced to be more willing to let other people help me. I hated telling people about my CF because I knew it made me "different." Not all my friends could handle all the details of my life. So I had to figure out who I could share things with. Some of them hated watching me do my treatments or poke my finger with a lancet to test my blood sugar levels. Some of them couldn't handle visiting me in the hospital or seeing me with an IV in my arm when I did home IV treatments. Others just took it in stride. You're not going to be able to share everything with everyone. But if you can find *one* person with whom you can be vulnerable, you're doing really well.

Our crosses will make our vulnerability visible to the world, no matter how hard we might try to hide them. We have to choose what we're going to do with that. Will we try to keep up the facade that everything is fine? Or will we allow people into our reality and help us carry it? Will we allow them the privilege of serving us, as Simon served Christ?

Questions along the Way of Your Cross

1. Have you been a Good Samaritan to someone in your life? What was that experience like?
2. Do you allow others to help you? Or do you insist that everything is fine and that you can do everything yourself? If you are reluctant to ask for help or accept it, journal about why.
3. What can you do today to allow yourself to show your vulnerability and allow others to serve you?

CHAPTER 6
BIG LITTLE THINGS

"You shall love the Lord your God with all your heart, and with all your soul, and with all your mind, and with all your strength." The second is this, "You shall love your neighbor as yourself." There is no other commandment greater than these.

—Mark 12:30–31

Unlike Simon, who is forced into carrying the cross, tradition tells us that Veronica comes to Jesus of her own free will. Nothing compels her except her own heart. She is moved by Jesus' suffering, and even though she cannot do much, she does what she can.

It's a small gesture, but one with impact. Jesus' face must have been coated with sweat and blood. I imagine most of us have had the experience of sweat or rain or snow getting into our eyes. It's not pleasant. How much worse was the mixture of blood and sweat (and maybe tears)? Veronica, like Mary at the wedding at Cana, sees a need and addresses it; she takes off her veil and presses it gently against Jesus' face.

Did she know Jesus? Maybe she knew *of* him. Perhaps she had heard his name or gone to listen to him preach. But Veronica does not appear in scripture, and legend tells us nothing more about her. If she really did exist, we can guess that she wasn't one of Jesus' friends—she probably didn't know him intimately, as did Mary, Martha, and Lazarus. He was little more than a stranger to her. Yet she does him this kindness because she is moved to do it. Her heart impels her forward.

But the question is, why? Why in the world would anyone do what Veronica did? Here was a man condemned to die, in excruciating pain. How would wiping his face help him at all? Jesus is just going to die anyway. Why take the risk of being harassed by the soldiers or the crowd?

Because of love. Veronica knew where Jesus was going; she knew he was going to die. And yet she wanted to make his last few hours on earth more comfortable. She wanted to do what she could to help him know that he was loved, even if it was only providing a tiny bit of comfort.

A Cup of Cold Water and a Smile

In the Gospel of Matthew, Jesus says, "Whoever gives even a cup of cold water to one of these little ones in the name of a disciple—truly I tell you, none of these will lose their reward" (Mt 10:42). We must learn to be comfortable with our own vulnerability, but we must also learn how to *respond* to the vulnerability of others. The "other" isn't just people we know. It's the golden rule: do unto others as you would have them do unto you. We're taught this from childhood, but many of us have forgotten just how powerful a small kindness can be.

We don't have to be intimately acquainted with people to be kind to them. Mother Teresa often told people to smile at one another. A smile is a small thing, as wiping someone's face is a small thing, but it can be surprisingly hard to do when we're wrapped up in our own day-to-day concerns. Do we smile at the barista who hands us our coffee, the teller at the bank, or the boy at the drive-through window? Or are we focused on finishing our transaction and getting on with our day?

A Life-Saving Visit

I met a lot of wonderful nurses and techs in my many hospital visits, but there are a few who really stand out. One of them is Rita Diewald, a pulmonary floor nurse who also lived in our neighborhood. Her daughter was my classmate, so our families knew each other. After my diagnosis, though, we all grew a lot closer. Rita was the one who went to my sixth-grade classroom and explained what CF was to my classmates and teachers. She came to our house to change the dressings for my IV lines, and she let me interview her for my high school research paper on CF. Besides being a great nurse, she was also a ton of *fun*. She has a huge, infectious laugh and energy that precedes her greeting, "How are you, sister?" followed by an all-enveloping hug.

Even when Rita wasn't my assigned nurse, she would visit me after her shift was over or before it started if I was in-house. She would sit with me, and we'd talk about all sorts of things—school, my parents and siblings, boys, theater (her daughter and I both loved theater), and the antics of her dog, Rosie. She would stay for a good hour just talking with me.

One night, her visit probably saved my life. She and I were talking, and I had to go to the bathroom, but I was attached to wires and a chest tube and thus needed help. So she helped me get up, get into the bathroom, and then resettled me back into the bed.

As I laid back against the pillows, I realized I couldn't breathe properly. I wasn't getting enough air. Rita immediately knew something was wrong. She quickly figured out that part of my lung may have collapsed, so in a calm, even voice, she explained that she was going to get the doctor, and I was to just keep breathing until she came back with some medicine.

Because she was there, I got immediate treatment. It was 9:30 at night (of course—these things never happen during the daytime!), but she called my parents, and things began to move. Her small decision to visit me turned out to be incredibly significant.

Rita was truly a Veronica for me that night. Yes, nursing is her job; she gets paid to take care of her patients. But that doesn't extend to off-hours visits, coming to my theater performances, or her daughter inviting my family and me to her birthday party. There are bonds of love there that go beyond service. And in that loving, she made things such as hospitalizations and chest tubes and being listed for transplant easier to handle.

Even if I *had* died that night, I would've died with my last human interaction being one of care and concern. The last face I would've seen would've been the face of someone who loved me. If you've been in the hospital, you can see the difference between nurses who care about their patients and nurses who treat patients as a thing to be dealt with. It's not a small difference.

Mother Teresa brought people off the street of Kolkata so they would not die alone. Did she cure them? Usually not. The people died anyway. But she saw Jesus in them and gave them a place of love, comfort, and care for their last few moments.

"You Did It to Me"

John Paul II brings to mind one of the focal points of the Gospel: the idea that what we do to others, we do to Jesus. He writes,

> These words about love, about actions of love, acts linked with human suffering, enable us once more to discover, at the basis of all *human sufferings, the same redemptive suffering of Christ*. Christ said, "You did it to me." He himself is the one who in each individual experiences love; he himself is the

> one who receives help, when this is given to every
> suffering person without exception. (SD 30)

Jesus says, "Truly I say to you, as you did it to one of the least of these my brethren, you did it to me" (Mt 25:40). We are Veronica every time we step outside ourselves and provide solace and succor to others who are suffering—even if *we* are suffering at the same time. We are called to think about others, to live beyond our own concerns and do what we can to smooth the road for our fellow travelers. We are not exempt from helping other people. Yes, there are times when we need people to help us. But we must also reach out to others with a smile, a kind word, or an after-hours visit.

Never underestimate the power of small actions. Their repercussions are much greater and last much longer than what we can see.

Questions along the Way of Your Cross

1. Can you recall a "small" gesture of kindness that meant a lot to you?
2. Do you always try to do the "big thing," or do you focus on doing something "small" for someone?
3. What small gesture can you make today to help someone who is struggling?

CHAPTER 7
DOWN AGAIN

The LORD upholds all who are falling,
and raises up all who are bowed down.

—Psalm 145:14

Even Simon's assistance is not enough to keep Jesus from falling
again. Every step brings him closer to the top of Calvary, but each
step also depletes his already low reserves. His battered body suc-
cumbs to its human weakness, and he falls again amid the jeers of
the crowd and the bite of Roman whips.

And unbelievably, he gets up again. With a breaking heart,
he still manages to struggle upward and continue toward Calvary,
because of his love for us.

Close to Jesus

If we give the suffering in our lives to God, he can use it to bring
us closer to him. Mother Teresa called this the "kiss of Jesus," being
so close to Jesus on the Cross that he could kiss you. And in theory,
that seems nice. Yes, I want Jesus to kiss me! Yes, I want to be *that*
close to God!

Until it happens. And continues. Until it's more than a week,
a month, or even a year of suffering. It's *years*. It's *decades*. You fall
once, get up, and tell yourself that it won't happen again, but then
it does. And as much as you don't want to, as convinced as you are
that you cannot, you have to get up or crawl, because what's the
alternative? Is there one?

"Life is pain, highness. Anyone who says differently is selling something," says the Dread Pirate Roberts in *The Princess Bride*. And we know this. We also know that this life leads to death. But what we don't know—what we have to choose to believe—is that death is not the end.

But that isn't a onetime thing. You never accept your cross just *once*, right? The marriage doesn't disintegrate in one day. Your mother doesn't die and you get over it at the wake. Pain and loss have echoes that last for the rest of your life sometimes, and you learn to walk with that pain—or the pain will burrow deep into your soul and twist it.

At times like this, we can long for death, because we begin to believe it could be a release from the pain we feel. At least if we die, it's over, right?

Well, not so fast. While it's good to remember that we will die and that heaven is our goal, we have work to do on earth. While escaping our crosses through death might seem desirable, it's not how life works. We have to face the cross (and carry it) on a daily basis. Sometimes, sure, we have days that are wonderful, and we can almost forget. But in the midst of suffering, the pain mocks and humiliates us. Have you ever felt that God is mocking *you*? You're not alone in that. The psalmist wrote, "My God, my God, why have you forsaken me?" (Ps 22:1), and Jesus quoted those words as he was dying on the Cross.

At one time or another, when part of us is dying, we ask that question too. Where is God now? Where is he when you have to drag the cross of suffering for an entire lifetime? Where is he when the stress piles up, and the bills, the paperwork, the commitments, and the loneliness? Where is God *really*? Where is he when everything seems to be ashes, when you are "poured out like water" and your strength is "dried up like a potsherd" (Ps 22:14, 15)?

Unleashing Hope

In the fall of 2001, I went to the emergency room with what I thought was pancreatitis, and I ended up spending two weeks in the ICU in a medically induced coma. The doctors couldn't figure out what was wrong with me. They prepared my parents for the worst. It wasn't until a brilliant ICU doctor dug deep and refused to write me off that she discovered I'd been infected with a bacteria that only *one other person in the world* had ever had. (Very odd things happen to me. It's my lot.)

In my coma, I had some very strange dreams, but I also experienced something I don't think was a dream. Somehow, in that suspended space, I knew that I could choose between life and death. I could just let go. It would be "quicker and easier than falling asleep," as J. K. Rowling says in *Harry Potter and the Deathly Hallows*.[1] It would require no effort. I just had to drift away.

But then, another thought invaded—*it wasn't my time*. My work wasn't done. Yes, it would be easy to let go, to die. But I was only nineteen, and God had more for me to do here. It was harder to choose life. But either because I'm stubborn or for some other reason, I did. I held on. That Thanksgiving I went home to my family, and in January, I returned to college.

I did not, however, return to life as it had been. Things were different. I was much weaker and would never be as strong as I had been before. I had learned that the body abandons you *rapidly* when you are lying flat for two weeks; I had to practice things such as sitting up in a chair and reaching my arms above my head. (Which hurts when you have chest tubes, folks. Not fun.)

John Paul II writes that "suffering . . . is always *a trial*—at times a very hard one—to which humanity is subjected" (SD 23). And I wasn't the only one subjected to this suffering; it affected my family, my friends at school, my professors, the doctors and nurses who knew and loved me, my parish family . . . all of us.

But in deciding to live—in deciding to do what Jesus did and get back up and carry the cross still farther—I also discovered hope. As John Paul II continues,

> To suffer means to become particularly *susceptible*, particularly *open to the working of the salvific powers of God*, offered to humanity in Christ. In him God has confirmed his desire to act especially through suffering, which is man's weakness and emptying of self, and he wishes to make his power known precisely in this weakness and emptying of self. (SD 23)

I had certainly emptied myself! But I had also been *saved*. I should have—and could have—been dead. But God saved me, continuing to do his work in me, because my story was not yet done.

Restarting my life was hard, yes. I was weak. I had eighteen credit hours of coursework to make up. I had to adjust to living at home again after enjoying the independence of dorm life. But in all of this, I also felt hope. Hope because I was *still alive*. Hope because I knew I had not yet fulfilled God's plan for me.

In reading the words of John Paul II, I found echoes of my own experience.

> Suffering . . . contains a special *call to the virtue* which man must exercise on his own part. And this is the virtue of perseverance in bearing whatever disturbs and causes harm. In doing this, the individual unleashes hope, which maintains in him the conviction that suffering will not get the better of

> him, that it will not deprive him of his dignity as
> a human being, a dignity linked to the awareness
> of the meaning of life. (SD 23)

Jesus got up, even though he was dehydrated and every cell in his body was probably screaming for him to stop. The Father's plan for him was not yet fulfilled. He knew he had work to do.

You also have work to do. This suffering? It will have an end. You might not be able to see it right now. Your prayer might be "Fix it *now*!" or "End this *now*!" But in this moment, you are given the virtues, the *strength*, to go on, to press on to the end even though the end is not in sight.

Choose to go on. Choose to live. Choose to trust. Choose to be open to hope.

Questions along the Way of Your Cross

1. Have you ever shouted to God, "Fix it!"? What drove you to that point? How did you feel after that?
2. Do you feel you can get angry at God? Why or why not?
3. Do you think there's a difference between "giving up" and "giving it up"? What do you think that difference might be?

CHAPTER 8
SURROUNDED

Therefore, since we are surrounded by so great a cloud of witnesses, let us also lay aside every weight and the sin that clings so closely, and let us run with perseverance the race that is set before us, looking to Jesus the pioneer and perfecter of our faith, who for the sake of the joy that was set before him endured the cross, disregarding its shame, and has taken his seat at the right hand of the throne of God.

Consider him who endured such hostility against himself from sinners, so that you may not grow weary or lose heart.

—Hebrews 12:1–3

Only St. Luke gives us Jesus' encounter with the women of Jerusalem, identifying them among those who have been following him. Unlike the rest of the jeering, taunting crowd, these women "wailing for him" (Lk 23:27). They didn't follow Jesus on the Way of the Cross to mock him for sport or out of curiosity. They followed because they mourned what was happening to him. Maybe they wanted him to see that there were people who still loved him. Maybe they had been so touched by his preaching that they felt compelled to follow this man to his death, to be with him, even though they didn't know him personally. At times, grief compels us to do things that might otherwise be considered irrational.

And Jesus rewards their efforts. He stops and speaks to them, giving them some of the scant words he manages to utter throughout his entire ordeal, on the way to his death. At first glance, what he says to them seems strange—almost apocalyptic. "Do not weep for me," he says, "but weep for yourselves and for your children" (Lk 23:28). How are these words supposed to be useful to them—or to us?

Weeping for the Women

First, it is striking that Jesus stops at all. At this point in his journey, Calvary is very close. Even though he knows what will happen to him on the hill, he must, at some level, *want* to reach the top.

But the women's sorrow must have been so evident—it must have made enough of an impression—that it merits another halt. Jesus reaches into himself and summons the resources needed to speak to them. He thinks about the women here, not himself: "Do not weep for me."

It's almost as if Jesus is saying, *Yes, my death—how it looks to you—is sad. But it will not end in sadness. It will end in glory. Pray that you and your children can follow me all the way to the glory beyond the cross. Pray that you will follow me all the way to heaven.*

In his death, Jesus "strike[s] at the root of evil, planted in the history of man and in human souls. . . . This work, in the plan of eternal love, has a redemptive character" (SD 16). Jesus sees the triumph that will be found on the other side of the Cross. He wants the women to see it too.

Reaching Outward

Have you noticed a strange thing about death? I have.

A person who is dying is often concerned about *others*, people who are *not* dying. My mother said she saw this in my grandfather. I've even noticed it in myself. At times when I was close to death, I worried about my parents, siblings, and friends, and less so about myself. Somehow, I knew I'd be OK, but I was concerned about those I would leave behind.

Before—and during—his Passion, Jesus thinks about *us*. He comforts *us*. And this is the same thing we see when those we love suffer, and even as we think about our own death. It's not just *all about us*. It's about the people we leave behind.

Suffering and pain can cause us to be selfish. It's not something we do on purpose, but it can happen. Grief can tie us up in knots, leading us to think only of *our* pain, *our* loss. But there is something about death, and our awareness of it, that makes us reach outward.

I don't know about you, but I can't stand it when people act unpleasantly because they're sick. I know this is a failing in me, and it's something I'm working to rectify. But in the back of my head is the voice that says, *I am almost* always *sick, and yet I'm not always mean to people.*

Even in suffering, we have to look outside ourselves. To me, that means thanking the nurses and doctors as they leave my hospital room, even if they weren't kind to me. It means smiling at receptionists, if at all possible. It means not screaming at incompetent lab techs or at the person in the parking garage who cannot park her car to save her life and is going to make me late for my appointment.

We can use our suffering as an excuse to be rude, selfish people, but that's not what Jesus did. And it's not what God wants us to do. With grace (and practice), we can learn to be outwardly directed, even in the midst of pain.

Are you wrapped up in your own pain? Or are you able to look outside yourself to what others may be suffering? Try to see the pain of others, and do what you can to assuage it.

A Good Death

When people talk about a "good death," this is what I think of—not the assisted-suicide, morphine-overdose sort of "good death," the one that offers to eliminate pain and suffering by prematurely ending life but a death that allows for things to be settled, put in place, perhaps made right, before the moment comes. For a Catholic, that would mean receiving a sacramental anointing, making that last confession, and receiving the Eucharist, if possible. It means forgiving and asking for forgiveness, letting people know how much they mean to you, and communicating all those important things we know we want to say. (Of course, we should do this *all the time*, not just when we're looking at death!)

A good death is one that is peaceful, prepared, and outwardly focused. It's also, however, inwardly rooted. Not that we become consumed with our own suffering; Jesus didn't do it, and we shouldn't either. Instead, we choose to look to those around us and think about them. Still, suffering is a unique call to personal penance and conversion. In fact, John Paul II says it "*must* [emphasis added] serve *for conversion*, that is, *for the rebuilding of goodness* in the subject, who can recognize the divine mercy in this call to repentance" (SD 12).

You could die right after reading this chapter. Just as I could die after writing it.

Are you prepared? Have you tried to rebuild goodness in your life?

An excellent way to do this is the practice of the Examen before bedtime. There are lots of ways to do it (see the Additional Resources for my favorite), but it always involves looking over your day and seeing what you did well and where you fell short and then praying an act of contrition. I just started doing this recently, and it's *very* (uncomfortably) illuminating.

The purpose of reviewing the day isn't self-flagellation. It's also to help us identify what we did well, not just missed opportunities and character weaknesses. The Examen prepares us for a good death, and it enables us to see how our actions affect others. It causes us to *think*, honestly and without dissembling, about how our actions cause either joy or pain in the world.

Questions along the Way of Your Cross

1. Do you practice a daily or weekly Examen? If not, consider starting the practice today using one of the resources listed in the back of the book.
2. What could you do to use what you are suffering to reach out to someone else?
3. In your experience with death, have you seen "good" deaths or "bad" deaths? What do you think makes the difference?

CHAPTER 9
IN THE DUST

> We are afflicted in every way, but not crushed; perplexed, but not driven to despair; persecuted, but not forsaken; struck down, but not destroyed; always carrying in the body the death of Jesus, so that the life of Jesus may also be made visible in our bodies.
>
> —2 Corinthians 4:8–10

Jesus is completely depleted. If he was a modern marathon runner, we'd say he had "hit the wall." In each of his previous falls, he still managed to get up, to struggle forward, and to continue carrying the Cross. But at this point, Simon and the Roman soldiers have to be doubting whether he is going to make it.

Extreme thirst, blood loss, and total exhaustion, combined with physical shock, are overwhelming him. He is outside the city gates, and Calvary is near. The end—his end—is closer than ever.

He *must* get there. But he has fallen yet again, and struggling to get up must seem pointless.

Surrender

Surrender is a word with a negative connotation. We generally don't want to give up; we don't like to be "quitters." At least, I don't. I want to be the responsible, dependable person. I don't want to run away when the going gets tough.

But when you're pushed to your limit, surrender starts to seem not only acceptable but also desirable. How easy it would be to

47

simply say, "That's it. I'm done." How freeing to lay down the burden, to stop caring, to just give up!

The appeal of surrender is undeniable, especially when we're sure things can't get any worse, and suddenly they do. Or when we think we can't get any lower, and we find ourselves looking up to ground level, from the bottom of a hole we didn't even see coming.

Who in their right mind wants to keep going, when everything seems to be conspiring to get you to quit?

Is God punishing me? you might ask. *Why does this keep getting worse? Where is God now that I'm lower than low and I don't see any way out?*

This is a good time to ask yourself, *Is God asking me to try to get out of this hole, or is he asking me to surrender my will to his?* Could God be asking me to accept this circumstance, this place where no victory is possible, where I see no light at the end of this tunnel . . . and trust him anyway?

What if realizing that you can't do this on your own and surrendering your will to God—giving him the whole messy situation, all the pain, all the emotion—is what God wants you to do?

Dark Nights

The worst time of day for me is night. When I'm stressed or sad or scared, nighttime is almost unbearable. It tends to be that way when I'm sick too. Nothing terrible ever happens when doctor's offices are *open*; have you noticed that? It's always at 2:00 a.m.

In my senior year of college, I began the long series of events that led to my name being placed on the United Network for Organ Sharing (UNOS) transplant waiting list. My condition was, to be charitable, not good. I graduated from college (on time, a miracle in itself) and had started a job with the Ohio State Senate, but I knew that it wasn't going to be long before my body would reach a critical phase. My health was in free fall. I was in the hospital for weeks at a time. I couldn't walk across a room. Brushing my teeth took a lot of effort. I slept like a cat, which is to say, more or less constantly. And underneath all this was the truth that for me to live, someone else had to die and that I might not be saved in time. My life could end at the age of twenty-three.

When you're waiting for an organ transplant, you are waiting for a life-changing phone call. It's like waiting for that boy you liked in high school to call you, except multiplied by about two hundred million. Every time the phone rings, it could be "the call." Every day that I *didn't* get the call made me a shade more desperate.

I had to keep it together during the day. I had work to do, and my siblings still lived at home. I couldn't go nuts in front of them or my parents. But at night, I lost it. I sobbed in my bed quietly, clinging to the hope that God *had not* abandoned me, that God *had a plan*, and that somehow this was all going to be *OK*, no matter *how* it turned out.

Fear of Death

I wasn't afraid of death; I was afraid of *dying*. I was afraid of the process, of how it would go, how my family would take it, how I could bear to tell my friends, and how heartbroken my grandparents would be.

St. Paul writes that "we are always being given up to death for *Jesus'* sake" (2 Cor 4:11, emphasis added), and that was something I meditated on during those long nights. This was my life. This was my path. This was how I was going to work out my salvation—and God knew the ending.

The only question that mattered was, did I trust him enough?

I had always been attracted to the idea of redemptive suffering, that somehow what we endure can be joined to Jesus' suffering. I thought I understood what John Paul II meant when he wrote, "To share in the sufferings of Christ is, at the same time, to suffer for the Kingdom of God. In the eyes of the just God, before his judgment, those who share in the sufferings of Christ become worthy of this Kingdom" (SD 21). My brain knew that this was true. My heart, however, had some problems with it.

I'm the person who writes out an itinerary when I travel, who picks out shops and restaurants and makes dinner reservations months ahead of time. To an extent, I was OK with not having a plan (because with CF, there is never a *plan*; everything can change in two minutes). But I also like to know how the story ends. I read *The Return of the King* before I saw the movie because I wanted to know how the series ended.

In this case, everything was out of my control. Every single thing. The only person who knew what was going to happen was God. I see now that I was being called to spiritual maturity. I began to pray more or less constantly. I prayed to make it to work without having to pull over on the highway because my stomach was in constant turmoil. I prayed to be able to get through a workday. I prayed that I'd be able to take a bath without becoming exhausted. I could not get through an hour without asking for divine assistance.

In this darkness, I was undergoing what John Paul II calls a "spiritual tempering . . . in the midst of trials and tribulations, which is the particular vocation of those who share in Christ's sufferings" (SD 23).

I'm sure you've experienced that in your life. You take three steps forward and two steps back, and you're doing it in darkness.

This darkness does not last.

It's hard to believe that when you're in the midst of it. But, as Samwise Gamgee said in the film version of *The Two Towers*, "Even darkness must past. A new day will dawn, and when the sun shines, it will shine out the clearer."

Jesus knows your feelings of wanting to hold on to where you are rather than reaching into the unknown. He knows the darkness and the doubt and the creeping feeling of intense fear that fills your stomach and your heart.

Give it to him. Cry out to him. But don't forget to listen for the answer. There will be one, even if it's in the "still small voice" (1 Kgs 19:12, RSV) that spoke to Elijah.

He has not abandoned you, but to find him, you must learn to abandon yourself. You must learn to surrender not just your situation but your whole life. Not to give up but to give *it* up.

Why not throw yourself into his arms? He is there to catch you when you fall.

He is with you in the dust.

Questions along the Way of Your Cross

1. How have you experienced falling? Do you find it harder or easier to get up again after you've fallen more than once?
2. Is there something you find difficult to surrender to God? What do you think might happen if you did?
3. How do you respond to another's weakness? How do you respond to your own weaknesses?

CHAPTER 10

STRIPPED

He said, "Naked I came from my mother's womb, and naked shall I return there; the Lord gave, and the Lord has taken away; blessed be the name of the Lord."

—Job 1:21

Jesus has reached Golgotha. Here, his journey carrying the Cross stops—but that doesn't mean that his suffering ends. It just takes a different shape.

The soldiers forcibly remove the garment he's wearing and also his loincloth. Jesus is completely naked before the crowd who has come to watch him die. There's no modesty, no dignity left to him now.

Unarmed

Being naked is a special sort of embarrassment. You can't hide anything—not your scars, birthmarks, or the jiggly parts that might make you cringe when you're in front of a dressing room mirror. There's no gorgeous clothing or fun accessory to take the attention away from you. Clothes protect us not only physically but also emotionally—we can hide in them in a variety of ways. We can use them to draw attention away from what we feel are the bad parts of us and focus on the good parts. It's like a magician's trick—Don't look here! Look here!

In the 2015 live-action version of *Cinderella*, one of the things that really struck me was the line, "The greatest risk any of us will take is to be seen as we truly are."

Cinderella had to reveal her real self to the prince—she wasn't a princess; she was a maid in her stepmother's house. She was terrified of how he would react. All of us can understand her trepidation because we've all been there. How will this person react to seeing the *true* me?

How much scarier is the idea of showing God our true selves when we come before him at the moment of our death? At that instant, there will be no way to hide from him. God knows everything about us, no matter how much we try to hide it. We can't run away from him, and we can't fool him. But we usually manage to push the thought aside and go on with our day. And if we sin, we know we can go to confession and start again. But in death, we can't do that. There's no way to hide, no way to *not* think about what's happening.

The good news is that God loves us *anyway*. We stand before him, stripped of all our pretense, and he still loves us. There's nothing he sees that repels him or makes him recoil. We're his precious children, and no matter how scarred, bruised, afraid, or ashamed we are, he still loves us, and he always will. His love for us is never-ending.

Created in Love

I'm not often ashamed of my body. I know people who are, who try to punish it and force it to obey. My body and I are often at odds—it often does things I don't want it to do. But generally, I like my body. There are times, however, when I try to cover what's "wrong" with it.

When I did courses of home IVs, I would often try to cover up the IV site, because no one really sees people walking around with IVs outside of a hospital. I used to get a lot of IV treatments in the summer, which meant that if I wanted to go swimming, I had to place plastic wrap over the IV site to keep it dry.

At the time, one of my friends had a pool that I would visit on hot summer days. As a seventeen-year-old, even among my best friends, I was a little embarrassed to have the IV be so visible, even under the plastic wrap. My friends didn't say anything, but one of their fathers did. "Where's the IV pole?" he joked as he came into the kitchen where we were eating some snacks after swimming.

My face burned red, and I didn't answer. I hated the attention that he'd drawn to me and the feeling that I wasn't "normal."

As I got more sick, and my veins continued to fail, I had a port-a-cath put in, like cancer patients have. It's about the size of a quarter, and it sits under my left collarbone. It's visible if you're looking for it. But when I weighed ninety pounds, it was *scarily* visible. I felt I had an alien communication device implanted under my skin and that *everyone* saw it. I was always trying to find new ways to cover it up in order to avoid questions and stares.

I know most people stare or make comments because they are reacting to something unfamiliar. As John Paul II said so well, "Human suffering evokes compassion; it also evokes *respect*, and in its own way *it intimidates*" (SD 4). Suffering is intimidating, and many people draw back from it.

This is true not only for visible physical deformity, scars, or oddities but also for emotional or hidden ones. Just think about how depression and anxiety are discussed. I've seen a therapist since I was sixteen, and I've taken antianxiety meds about that long. And yet, I've had people tell me that I just need to "think positive" and "be happy" or, my favorite, "pray more." When you expose your vulnerability to people, and they fire back platitudes such as "be happy" or "pray more," that's discouraging. It's also a bit enraging.

I know that praying more isn't an answer to changing brain chemistry. Sometimes you need more than prayer. You need doctors and medications and procedures. You need medicine. And Jesus never tries to pacify us with a thrown-off "Well, you just need to *believe more*."

In our vulnerability, in the times when we stand naked before the crowd of people and share our souls and bare our true selves, not everyone will be able to respond graciously.

But God, who created you *perfectly*, who has known you from the time you were a zygote and created you unique among everyone else in the world who has ever lived and will ever live, loves you *completely*. No matter what your body looks like, no matter what you try to hide—God sees you, loves you, and wants *you*. Just the way you are. You are enough, without accessories.

Questions along the Way of Your Cross

1. When have you felt the most vulnerable or exposed in your life? What was the situation? How did you feel during it and afterward?
2. Do you feel that God loves you just the way you are? Or is this a concept you struggle with? Why?
3. How has God revealed himself to you? What was your response?

CHAPTER 11
IT HURTS

"Very truly, I tell you, when you were younger, you used to fasten your own belt and to go wherever you wished. But when you grow old, you will stretch out your hands, and someone else will fasten a belt around you and take you where you do not wish to go." (He said this to indicate the kind of death by which he would glorify God.) After this he said to him, "Follow me."

—John 21:18–19

After being forcibly stripped, Jesus lies down upon the wood of the Cross and is nailed to it. These nails were driven into nerve bundles that led to the fingers and toes to cause the maximum amount of pain and suffering. Every time the crucified person moved, the agony of the initial nailing was revisited—and the victim had to move in order to breathe. Jesus had no way to relieve his pain.

Fear and Pain

When people are asked why they're afraid of death, one of the things that always comes up is the idea of being in pain with no way to relieve it. Physical pain is frightening because most people don't experience high-level pain over extended periods of time throughout their lives. Death, they expect, will involve sickness or injury, which more often than not involves pain, either from symptoms or from the things used to *treat* the symptoms (such as tests, procedures, surgeries, or other medical interventions).

And I get that. I really do. I'm not going to tell you there isn't a legitimate reason to be afraid of pain because, to be blunt, being in pain is not fun. It hurts.

Pain is an unavoidable part of life, whether it's physical pain, mental pain, or emotional pain. There's no way to live a human life *without* experiencing one, some, or all of these things. But that doesn't mean pain is totally bad. It's not *fun*, but it's not always bad. Look at what Jesus says to Peter in the scripture verses at the beginning of this chapter: Peter's death would *glorify God*.

St. Peter was crucified upside down. Jesus knew that's how he would die. And yet he still tells Peter that his death will bring *glory*. The way we live our lives can bring glory to God too—even in moments of agony.

You Don't Have to Like It

One of my least favorite medical tests is something called a pH probe test. Essentially, the test is designed to test the acid content of your stomach, to determine whether you have acid reflux (aka heartburn). In people with CF or other lung diseases, reflux can cause or aggravate respirator problems, so it's important to see if this condition exists.

This test is, quite honestly, horrible. A slim probe, about the diameter of a piece of spaghetti (but about three feet long) is pushed up your nose, down your throat, and into your stomach, with the end of the probe taped to your face. It's placed quickly, and it hurts. A lot. The probe is attached to a small device that you wear around your waist for twenty-four hours. It tracks when you eat so the probe knows when to measure acid levels. You're supposed to "eat normally," which is hard to do when you've got something foreign (and highly irritating!) in your esophagus.

I knew the probe test lasted for "only" twenty-four hours. That didn't help me during the time the stupid probe was stuck in my stomach and taped to my face.

But thinking about Jesus, I remembered two things:

1. He knew excruciating pain, so he could relate to what I was enduring, and
2. I did not have to be happy about this while I was suffering.

That second point is important. Accepting suffering, pain, or death doesn't mean loving every minute of it. God doesn't expect us to be happy all the time, especially when we're suffering. The Christian life is a good one, but it isn't a lifetime of sunny days at Disney World. Sometimes it's pain, it's nails driven into flesh, it's agonizing emotional devastation, it's being unable to breathe as you lay limp on a gurney, and it's the demons of depression prowling around your brain and telling you that everyone would be better off without you.

Following Christ

John Paul II reminds us that Jesus was "sensitive to every human suffering, whether of the body or of the soul" (SD 16). He healed many people of physical afflictions while he ministered on earth. And he still heals people now, sometimes miraculously.

But not everyone gets that cure. Not everyone, as it were, can come down from the cross of pain. Sometimes there is no relief, no cure, no miracle, and no voice from the heavens. What do you do then?

Jesus was taunted as he was nailed to the Cross: "If you are the Son of God, come down from the cross" (Mt 27:40). These taunters echo Satan's temptation of Christ in the desert (cf. Luke 4:1–13).

We hear the same voices today. *If God was* really *good . . . if he* really *loved you . . .*

We are called to follow Christ. When we do, we will experience the Cross in all its pain and desolation, not just the Resurrection and the glory. I had a moment of that while writing this chapter, when my doctor's office called to tell me I have to see yet another specialist. *Really, God?* I fumed as I packed up my things to run errands. *Another doctor? More specialists? Really? Can't I get a break here?*

But like Peter, I have to follow Jesus where he leads me, even if it isn't where I want to go. If I really love Jesus—and I do—then this is what I must do. It's what *you* must do as well. We might kick and scream about it, roll our eyes, or grumble, but the test is what we *do*, not necessarily how we first *react*.

If you're kicking and yelling and complaining, do it loudly and get it out of your system. Then look at what's being asked of you. It might be to open your hands for the nails.

But don't fear what *might* happen. We don't know what God will ultimately ask of us. It might lead to us drawing back, afraid of the pain, afraid of the nails. Sometimes I've cowered before the mountain of what I thought God was asking me. But the only way to finish it is to take the first step—and that can be to open your hands and go where God is leading you, even if the path leads us through a place of pain. God might be bringing you to glory.

Questions along the Way of Your Cross

1. Do you feel the presence of God more or less in your moments of suffering?
2. Does the idea of not knowing how or when you'll die make the idea of death scarier for you?
3. Have you ever been angry with God? Do you think it's OK to express anger to God?

CHAPTER 12
THE LAST BREATH

Who will separate us from the love of Christ? Will hardship, or distress, or persecution, or famine, or nakedness, or peril, or sword? . . . No, in all these things we are more than conquerors through him who loved us. For I am convinced that neither death, nor life, nor angels, nor rulers, nor things present, nor things to come, nor powers, nor height, nor depth, nor anything else in all creation, will be able to separate us from the love of God in Christ Jesus our Lord.

—Romans 8:35, 37–39

This is the end of Jesus' life.

Here, on a wooden Cross, with only his mother, one disciple, Mary Magdalene, and a few women, Jesus' life ends. The crowds who cried out "Hosanna!" when he entered the city are replaced by those who shouted "Crucify him!" The rest of his apostles have fled, and the one who betrayed him has died by suicide. This Jesus is the man who performed miracles, who taught with authority, and who said he was the beloved Son of God. Now, on a Friday afternoon, he hangs between two thieves, dead on a hill outside Jerusalem. Jesus had spoken so eloquently of kingdoms, of God's love, and of what was in store for those who followed him. Is that all over now that he's dead? Was it ever real?

Little Deaths

You will physically die once in your life. But before that moment, there are so many "little deaths" that can influence the course of your life.

As children, most of us have dreams about what we want to be when we grow up, but they eventually fade or we realize they're unrealistic. I wanted to be a ballerina as a kid, but I'm ridiculously uncoordinated. So that dream went by the wayside, and I can't say I was too broken up about it. I'm sure you've had that experience too. Most of the time we don't mourn these forgotten childhood dreams because better things—or things that were more suited to our talents or temperaments—came along.

But what about those *good* dreams, the realistic ones we hope for and work toward? What happens when they're taken from us too? We experience death on a smaller scale and all the finality, loss, and grief that goes with it.

Dreams

Ever since I was a little girl, I've wanted to be a wife and mother. That's really all I wanted to do. I wanted a husband and at least five kids. I love children. I love the huge family gatherings we had with my mom's family; she's one of eight kids. I was committed to being a good mom.

My doctors had been telling me for years that I might be able to have one child. Women with CF aren't often *encouraged* to get pregnant (or at least they weren't back then), but if you were healthy enough, you could try.

My doctors attempted to tell me, gently, that I wasn't healthy enough. But I focused on maybe having *one* child. My body could do that, right? Not five, but hey, I could still be a mom!

Then I had my transplant. You *can* get pregnant after an organ transplant, but it carries its own risks. But then I entered menopause: at thirty-six. There's now no way, short of divine intervention, that I'll be able to have my own biological children.

I'm also single. It's hard, when you're Catholic, to find men who share your faith and who are willing to develop a deep, loving relationship with a woman who can't give them any children. I haven't found a man like that yet. So in addition to mourning the fact that I will never be a biological mother, I have to accept the possibility that I might never be a wife.

Family life is a *good* thing. It is what most women and men were created for—to love one another, to get married, and to have families. And I don't have a family of my own. Sometimes I'm so jealous of people who do that I can't see straight, even though I know that marriages aren't always sunshine and roses and soft-focus Instagram photos of little kids in a sunny meadow.

I'm a classically trained singer. I've always loved theater and music. My first "performance" was when I was three years old, playing Snow White for the parent performance at my preschool, because I knew all the words to "Someday My Prince Will Come." (I had stage fright. The performance wasn't as great as it should've been. I got over that eventually.) I was bitten by the theater bug early. Post-transplant, I had the lung function I needed to sing *better* than I ever had before. I was really excited.

And then I had to be on medications to beat an infection. And those medications slowly destroyed my hearing. Now, I'm grateful to be alive and hearing impaired rather than dead with great hearing. Still, it's eternally frustrating to have to give up a lot of my musical outlets. I still play and sing, mostly for myself, and I've done some community and regional musicals, but it's not the same. I'm not nearly as confident as I used to be. I miss being able to hear everything. It's another death. It's another thing I had to give up.

Difficult Yeses

Yes, I'm alive. But being alive doesn't mean there aren't moments of intense sadness over forfeiting things that I've always wanted to do, things that gave me joy and purpose and happiness. Sometimes I'm afraid I'll have to give up something else I love before I die. I don't know if I could handle that, to be honest.

I've had to let big dreams die and turn things that feel like failures and disappointments over to God again and again. I've said yes to whatever he gives me, even when it's ridiculously difficult, and sometimes I'm *angry* about having to say yes. Because what other option is there—saying, "No, God"?

OK. That's an option. But it doesn't lead anywhere good. What happens when we say no to God, when we deny his plan? It might feel good in the short run. But the consequences are dire.

If Jesus had said, "No, God," he wouldn't have died on his Cross. There would be no weeping at the foot of the Cross, no death, no taunting, no jeers, and no suffering. He'd be back in Nazareth with his mother or with his apostles in the countryside. This horrible and excruciating death wouldn't be happening to him.

But then—where would we be?

I've learned that saying yes, even through clenched teeth in a whisper, is better than saying no to God. Why? Because even when you're saying it amid a torrent of tears as you're curled up in bed and you have no idea how this yes can lead to anything good, God is there. On the Cross, on Good Friday, Jesus felt abandonment. He felt the loss of God. He is the only one who can really understand the way you feel.

I don't know how God will make use of the difficult yeses that I've given him in my life. But I have his word that he will.

Dead End

The Cross looks like failure. Our lives can look like failure too. When our dreams are broken and denied and rejected all around us, we may think this is all a *mess*, an irrevocable defeat. We wonder, *What in the world is God doing? How can this be good? How can even God make this good?*

In Christ's suffering, there is an opening for us to join *our* suffering to his. In the same way, our little deaths can be added to his as well. This doesn't mean our redemption isn't complete. But it does mean we can actively participate in salvation. As John Paul II writes,

> Christ achieved the Redemption completely and to the very limits but at the same time he did not bring it to a close. In this redemptive suffering, through which the Redemption of the world was accomplished, Christ opened himself from the beginning to every human suffering and constantly does so. . . .
>
> The mystery of the Church—that body which completes in itself also Christ's crucified and risen body—indicates at the same time the space or context in which human sufferings complete the sufferings of Christ. (SD 24)

God takes all my hard yeses, all your hard yeses, all the things we've given up, the dreams that have died, the things we wanted, and the plans we've had to put aside—he takes all we give him and gathers it up into the world's redemption. Will we ever know exactly how?

No. We just trust that he *does*. Nothing we suffer is wasted if we give it to God—no dead dream is really gone or lost—because nothing that is good is lost in Christ.

It might be hard to see it, but salvation and glory are coming for us too.

Questions along the Way of Your Cross

1. What dreams or aspirations have you had to give up? How has this shaped your character or the direction of your life?
2. What can you do today to unite the losses you have experienced with the saving death of Jesus?
3. How do you handle "little deaths"? Is it the same or different from how you respond to bigger deaths?

CHAPTER 13
UNBURDENED

But we have this treasure in clay jars, so that it may be made clear that this extraordinary power belongs to God and does not come from us. We are afflicted in every way, but not crushed; perplexed, but not driven to despair; persecuted, but not forsaken; struck down, but not destroyed; always carrying in the body the death of Jesus, so that the life of Jesus may also be made visible in our bodies. For while we live, we are always being given up to death for Jesus' sake, so that the life of Jesus may be made visible in our mortal flesh. So death is at work in us, but life in you.

—2 Corinthians 4:7–12

The physical pain is over now.

The body of Jesus is taken down from the Cross. It was not necessary to hasten his death by breaking his legs. Still, a soldier pierces his side with a lance—one final wound (see John 19:34).

After he's taken down from the Cross, the hands that touch him are the hands of those who loved him. The Bible doesn't elaborate, but I like to think that Jesus' body was given to Mary. Once again, Mary cares for her beloved son. But unlike all those other times—when she held him to her breast, when she hugged him, and when she took him out of his bath—there is no smile. Her beloved son's eyes are closed, and he is gone. She can only remember.

Risking Love

Death is a heavy thing. The body is heavy. Grief is heavy. There are the burdens of what ifs—things unsaid, things undone. In Jesus' life, he had the chance to speak to the people he loved best—his disciples, his mother—before he died. Nothing was left undone or unsaid. We aren't always so fortunate. We blithely think there will be all the time in the world to say and do the things we want to do for those we love or to ask forgiveness for things we've done (or to grant that forgiveness to others). Death is always in the distant future—until it's not.

And along the way of our own crosses, we can let impatience and anger shatter the delicate web of our relationships. We can strike out in anger, in fear, or in grief and hurt the people we love the most. Or we can do the opposite and retreat into ourselves thinking that we are a burden to those we love, that we are weighing them down with crosses that are not theirs. We think we can spare them grief or pain. But we can't.

Love is always messy. It's always, in a sense, a burden because it means we care about another person, someone else who can get sick or die. That someone may become hurt or injured—physically, mentally, or emotionally. That someone may even hurt us.

But when we love, we open ourselves up to pain and accept the risk. We know that love isn't just the bride and groom at the altar, resplendent in happiness. It's also the difficult marriage; the mother holding her sobbing daughter when she's had a terrible day of being bullied at school; the father praying for his child outside the ICU doors; and the friend listening to you pour out your grieving heart.

Every relationship on this planet will end in death. We will be physically removed from one another. All of us will die—and that will cause suffering for those who love us. There is tremendous pain in that realization. But is it better to avoid the pain by never loving someone else?

Burdens and Gifts

One of my deepest insecurities is the idea that I am a burden to my family, that my family's lives would be better if I just didn't exist. My siblings would've gotten more attention. My parents would have more money. My grandparents wouldn't have worried so much about me and instead delighted in their twenty-four other grandchildren.

Recently, while my parents and I were slogging through another never-ending pile of government and medical paperwork, I burst into tears at the kitchen table.

"What's wrong?" My father asked.

I blubbered out, "I'm such a pain to you. I make your lives so hard!" (Even writing this, tears are coming to my eyes.)

My parents looked at each other and then hugged me. "You are not a pain," my father said. "This is a pain," he said pointing to the papers, "but you are not. You're our daughter, and we love you. We wish that all this was easier for you."

Then my mother told me that when she and my father were married in 1979, they hoped to begin having kids soon. They were young by today's standards—they had just turned twenty-three—but they wanted a family. Every month, they waited for my mother to conceive, and it just wasn't happening. When I was born in April 1982, I was a gift, an answered prayer. Even though I was the color of a Smurf with an Apgar score of two and had to be sent to the special care nursery, my parents were overjoyed at my arrival.

Service through Suffering

Even though *On the Christian Meaning of Human Suffering* (*Salvifici Doloris*) was written in 1984, when I was two years old, there are passages that make me feel that John Paul II is speaking directly to me—especially when he writes about feeling like a burden.

> A source of joy is found in the *overcoming of the sense of the uselessness of suffering*, a feeling that is sometimes very strongly rooted in human suffering. This feeling not only consumes the person interiorly, but seems to make him a burden to others. The person feels condemned to receive help and assistance from others, and at the same time seems useless to himself. The discovery of the salvific meaning of suffering in union with Christ *transforms* this depressing *feeling*. Faith in sharing in the suffering of Christ brings with it the interior certainty that the suffering person "completed what is lacking in Christ's afflictions"; the certainty that in the spiritual dimension of the work of Redemption *he is serving*, like Christ, *the salvation of his brothers and sisters*. Therefore he is carrying out an irreplaceable service. (SD 27)

Do I always feel I'm carrying out an "irreplaceable service"? Well, no. But then again, that's life, especially the spiritual life. We don't always feel the highs of prayer and total union with Jesus. We have ups and downs. And in the downs, we need to be told, *you matter. Your life is not a waste.*

Whenever I feel I'm a burden to my family, I sit down and look at photographs. I see myself with my godson, Ryan. I see myself with my siblings on Christmas morning as my brother and I bury our sister Melanie in wrapping paper. I see Dad sitting on the deck of our rented condo in the Outer Banks. I see Mom holding me as a toddler beside her parents' Christmas tree. I see us laughing. I see our *family*. Yes, sometimes it's a hard life. There were the Christmases I spent on a drip of TPN and lipids to keep my body weight above a hundred pounds. There were years we missed traveling to Pittsburgh for Thanksgiving because I was in the hospital and weddings I missed because I was doing home IVs and couldn't travel.

But over all that is the *joy*.

"It is suffering, more than anything else, which clears the way for the grace which transforms human souls," John Paul II writes (SD 27). And that grace can be experienced in the moments of joy, of happiness, of communion with God and my family.

Every person we love will also bring us sadness. Death and loss are the opposite side of the coin of joy and love. We can't have one without the other.

As Mary receives the body of Jesus at the foot of the Cross, I imagine she feels the weight of her tears rolling down her cheeks. But she also knows that grief is the price she's paying for having her little boy, her son, her love, in her life.

Questions along the Way of Your Cross

1. Have you ever felt like deadweight to your friends or family? Have you been able to process these feelings?
2. Is there someone in your life who feels they are a burden to you? What can you do today to reassure them?
3. What are your remains? What would you leave behind if you died today?

CHAPTER 14
ASLEEP

A windstorm arose on the sea, so great that the boat
was being swamped by the waves; but he was asleep.
And they went and woke him up, saying, "Lord, save
us! We are perishing!"

—Matthew 8:24–25

During his Passion, Jesus' friends stood by helpless, unable to do anything to assuage his pain. But now that he is dead, they are free to act in love. Joseph of Arimathea buys a linen shroud, asks Pilate for permission to take Jesus' body away, and offers his own new tomb for burial. Nicodemus brings aloes and spices, which are used to cleanse, anoint, and perfume the body of the Lord they loved (see John 19:39).

Imagine the care they must have used in wrapping his body, which was so bloody and beaten and torn, with linen. I envision the women sponging off the blood, removing the crown of thorns, and cleaning his hair with attention and care. The time was short, but they wouldn't omit a single kindness, not for the one they loved. This was all that they could give him now.

They laid him in the new tomb and then went away, hearts heavy with loss.

They may have heard Jesus prophesy that he would rise again. But did that lessen their grief now? I'm guessing it probably didn't.

Looking for Answers

On Holy Saturday, there is no Mass. No sacraments are given, unless it's an emergency. The church is waiting—and we wait too at those moments in our journeys when everything is silent.

Every prayer is answered. My childhood pastor once said that God answers every prayer with "yes," "no," or "not right now." And that's generally how it goes, right? You either get the job, or you don't. The baby is conceived or isn't. The sick person lives or dies.

But what about the times when the answer is so long in coming that it seems there is no answer at all? What is God waiting for? He sees your anguish, your suffering, and your pain. And yet . . . he remains silent.

This is the silence of the tomb. At this point, you may find yourself wanting *any* answer, as long as it's *immediate*, rather than having to bear this silence one more second.

True, Jesus is there. But it may not be enough for us to know that Jesus is in the boat with us. We want him to *do something*. How many times in our lives does it seem as if Jesus is asleep—or dead—while we are perishing?

Thy Will Be Done

Waiting for an organ transplant is hard, on multiple levels. First, you feel terrible (obviously). I was forcing myself to go to work, but my "work" mostly consisted of sitting at my desk and answering the phone. My life consisted of work (if I was able to get myself ready that morning), IV meds, forcing some food into me, and sleeping, sometimes fourteen hours a day.

I was listed for transplant at the end of May 2005 and spent the entire month of June in the hospital. To receive a transplant, you have to be sick enough to need one but strong enough to survive the surgery and recovery period. This hospitalization was to get me as strong as possible, to pump my tiny body full of calories, and to let my body rest and prepare for the surgery that was—hopefully—ahead.

Second, I knew that I would either wait for a long time, or not long at all. Because I have a rare blood type (AB+) and I'm short (five-two at the time of transplant), I'd probably have to get lungs that were bigger than my own and have the surgeon trim them down. These things were either a blessing or a curse, and we did not yet know which.

Third—and probably most importantly—I knew that in order for me to live, someone else had to die. If I was to hear the life-giving words I was hoping for, others would hear words that would break their hearts and plunge them into grief.

In that situation, your prayer takes on a strange form. It's not like rooting for the Steelers to kick the Patriots' butts in the AFC championship game. I knew that my life was dependent on someone else's death. My prayer became—it had to become—"*Lord, thy will be done*." Any other prayer just seemed selfish. I couldn't pray for someone else to die. And how could God grant that prayer anyway? "Lord, please take someone away so I can stay"? That prayer couldn't cross my lips.

"Thy will be done" is an excruciatingly difficult prayer to pray. If you've ever really prayed that prayer, you know how hard it is. The Our Father takes on an entirely new dimension, because "thy will be done" is what actually *has to happen*. It's the bare-bones recognition that God's will—not mine—is what happens in the end.

Emphatic Silence

As I prayed, I waited. The way this particular prayer would be answered would be unmistakable—the phone would ring. I slept with my cell phone every night. You have to understand, this was 2005. Cell phones were still pretty new technology, and there weren't any smartphones yet. My cell phone was a tiny, navy blue Nokia with a black-and-white screen, and the whole thing was the size of my hand. So sleeping with your cell phone was . . . well, weird, at the time.

But everyone in my family did because, when "the call" came, we had to move fast. We would have to be at the hospital within a few hours. All of us jumped whenever any phone rang—house line, Dad's BlackBerry, and my cell phone. Every call could be *the call*.

And every time the phone rang, that May, that June . . . it wasn't what we were waiting for.

Waking up in the morning and seeing that no one had called during the night made my heart plunge fifty feet. It meant that more time had passed, and I was dying by inches. I didn't have time to waste. Every morning, I felt as C. S. Lewis did, after his wife, Joy, had died: "But go to Him when your need is desperate, when all other help is vain, and what do you find? A door slammed in your face, and a sound of bolting and double bolting on the inside. After that, silence. You might as well turn away. The longer you wait, the more emphatic that silence will become."[1]

A Calling

At this point in my life, I understood physical suffering as part of my vocation. Yours might be emotional, mental, or spiritual—we know there are thousands of ways to suffer and millions of ways to carry a cross. But for me, living (literally) in a body of death was the shape of my vocation.

I didn't have to accept this vocation. I could've fought against it, asked, "Why me?" and been filled with rage. But I didn't. I'm not entirely sure why I didn't. Even when it felt as if there was no answer to my prayers, even when I thought about impending death, I believed that Christ understood. As John Paul II notes, "Christ through his own salvific suffering is very much present in every human suffering, and can act from within that suffering by the powers of his Spirit of truth, his consoling Spirit" (SD 26).

God had prepared me for this. Even in the silence of waiting, I knew this. This was my life, and this was what I was being called to do. I would carry my cross to the end, just as all of us are called to carry our crosses, even in the times when we feel we are doing it alone. If my life was only a few days from its end, then it was going to end with me clinging to God and doing what he asked of me.

"When the first great chapter of the Gospel of suffering is written down," John Paul II writes, "simultaneously another great chapter of this Gospel unfolds through the course of human history. This chapter is written by all those *who suffer together with Christ*, uniting their human sufferings to his salvific sufferings" (SD 26).

You and I are called, even when God is silent and we feel there is no answer to our prayers, to proclaim this chapter of human history. We wait for the second coming of Christ—we wait for our own resurrection. And as we do this, we show the world that even when God appears to be silent, we will still love him. We will still follow him. We will still be faithful as we wait.

Questions along the Way of Your Cross

1. What's the hardest thing you've ever had to wait for? How did this time feel, spiritually? If you're still waiting, how does it feel?
2. What is your vocation? How would you describe it? Have you fully embraced it?
3. Have you entrusted your death—and your life—to God? How could you place yourself completely in his hands?

EPILOGUE
NEW LIFE

And I heard a loud voice from the throne saying,

"See, the home of God is among mortals.
He will dwell with them;
they will be his peoples,
and God himself will be with them;
he will wipe every tear from their eyes.
Death will be no more;
mourning and crying and pain will be no more,
for the first things have passed away."

And the one who was seated on the throne said, "See,
I am making all things new."

—Revelation 21:3–5a

Was there anything special about that Sunday morning?

As Mary Magdalene and the other women made their way to the tomb, their hearts were still heavy. Maybe the initial, devastating shock of Friday was gone, but they were still in pain. The day was only special to them because it offered them a last chance to say goodbye. There was still one thing left to do for Jesus.

It wasn't until the women reached the tomb and saw the inexplicable—the stone rolled away, the tomb empty—that the day changed.

Jesus was gone. Where could his body be? Had someone taken him away? Why?

But then—the gift. The best of all good news. He is not here; he is risen!

In St. John's gospel, Mary Magdalene is given the wondrous gift of an encounter with her beloved, risen Lord. There he is—his body, so beaten and abused, now fully glorified! How shocked, how amazed, how *joyful* Mary must have felt! Everything that had turned her life upside down was right side up again. He hadn't abandoned her. He hadn't left her alone. He had kept his promise. Her Lord was alive!

An ordinary Sunday suddenly became the day when everything was made new and became the best day of all. Isn't that true in our lives? The day that will change everything can be such a simple day, one with nothing exceptional about it.

Tears of Joy

The happiest moments of my life have happened on completely ordinary days. In fact, they were often days that, in other respects, weren't that great.

The day I received my transplant call was a Sunday. My parents, in a drastic attempt to get me off the couch, enticed me with a trip to the local shopping area. (I'm not that shallow, guys, but I do like to shop!) I went more to make them happy than to make myself happy. We had dinner at the local pub, and I pushed my fish sandwich around on my plate. Inside, I just wanted to go home.

As twilight fell, we decided to watch a movie in the family room. I was taking my evening meds and trying to gather my courage to call my boss and tell her I'd miss work tomorrow—*again*. (My boss was completely understanding of my situation, but I *hated* the idea that I was letting her down, even if that was only in my own head.) I'd only been awake for five hours or so, but I was exhausted. Getting up the stairs to my bedroom seemed impossible. Getting downtown tomorrow morning? Out of the question.

And then my cell phone rang. It was 8:45 p.m.

Karen, my transplant coordinator, was on the other end. "We have lungs for you," she said.

With those five words, everything changed.

Hopelessness became . . . hope. Sadness, weariness? Gone.

Suddenly, there was a chance at life.

At around 6:00 a.m. on July 11, 2005, I was taken back to the OR at Columbus Children's Hospital. Eleven hours later, I was out of surgery and in the cardiothoracic ICU. In early August, I was discharged.

I went home—alive. Well. Thriving. (Well, maybe not exactly thriving, I was still recovering from major surgery!) But on discharge day, that seemed a minor point. I could breathe!

There were tears, but they were tears of joy. They were the tears of prayers answered.

Ever Better

Think about the most perfect moments of your life for a second. Really bring them to life in your head. Where were you? Who was with you? What were you doing?

For me, it's a collage of moments.

Visiting the Outer Banks for the first time with my best friend, Tiffany.

Hearing Johnny Gilbert, the *Jeopardy!* announcer, say my name as we taped my episode of the long-running game show.

Receiving a standing ovation at the end of a performance of *Les Misérables*.

Eating pizza in Epcot's Italy Pavilion with my dad.

Watching my siblings get married.

Telling my parents I had a book contract.

But no matter how perfect all these moments were—heaven is going to be infinitely better.

By now, you know I love C. S. Lewis. At the end of *The Last Battle*, the final book in the Narnia series, Lewis writes, "All their life in this world and all their adventures in Narnia had only been the cover and the title page: now at last they were beginning Chapter One of the Great Story which no one on earth has read: which goes on for ever: in which every chapter is better than the one before."[1] That's what heaven is: the great, ongoing story, a story that just gets better all the time.

Because you have known suffering, your joy will be that much deeper. I promise you. I have experienced this in my own life. All the rejections, the setbacks, the hardship and disappointments—when the goal is reached, it is infinitely sweeter. How much truer will this be of heaven? The hope of heaven is always before us.

Glorious Scars

But in heaven, we will also have our battle scars.

What? Hang on a second. That doesn't sound like joy and glory, Emily.

Oh, but it will be.

When Jesus was resurrected, the marks of all he'd endured were still there. That's how the disciples knew they were seeing Jesus. Glory doesn't erase everything that came before.

Jesus' scars are *glorious*. And so are ours. When I see the scar on my forehead from skin cancer surgery or the heavily marked skin graft scar on my right arm, I don't see them as things to be ashamed of, to cover up, or to "fix." They are proof of survival and endurance. Yes, in heaven we will have glorified bodies. And no, the Church doesn't specifically say what those bodies will be like.

But I think that, for all the beauty, some mark of earth's pain will remain, as a *memento vitae*—a remembrance of *life*, the evidence of a battle fought and won. Maybe that's how we'll know each other. Like the end of *Beauty and the Beast*, when Belle only recognizes the handsome stranger before her when she looks in his eyes, our scars might be what identify us as *us*.

But while we're here on earth, we can learn to see our scars as beautiful. They aren't ugly because they mean we have survived. They are tokens of bravery. They are *glorious*! (That doesn't mean I show my transplant scars to anyone who asks though!)

With all we've endured, all we've suffered, and with all our scars, we can go *home*. And we can embrace death simply as the way we get there—the train we take, or the plane we catch. We can enter heaven with our battle-wearied bodies, knowing we were victorious, because Jesus was. And we can hope to hear "well done, good and faithful servant."

In receiving a transplant, I had escaped death—for now. I know that some day, death will come, and my life on earth will be over. But at the same time, a new story will begin.

Remembering that we will die is just another way of recalling that there is a whole new kind of life beyond death. Jesus promises us a new heaven and a new earth, with a place prepared for us. In this place, there are no more tears or sadness, and everything—including our bodies—will be made new.

ACKNOWLEDGMENTS

First and foremost, to my immediate family: my parents, Carmen and Michele DeArdo, and my siblings, Bryan DeArdo and Melanie McDonald.

To the doctors of Nationwide Children's Hospital's Pulmonary and Lung Transplant departments, especially Dr. Karen McCoy, Dr. Steve Kirkby, Dr. Don Hayes, and Dr. Richard Shell. Your expertise and sheer determination to find answers kept me alive in order to write this.

To the nurses of Nationwide Children's Hospital's Pulmonary and Transplant floors. You gave beyond the call of duty on a regular basis, even doing cartwheels in the hallway and smuggling dogs onto the floor (before therapy dogs were a thing!) to keep me entertained and laughing. Thank you for your dedication, optimism, and brilliance.

To Sarah Baumgardner, Andrea Burton, Mary Parker, Suellen Kasiara, Laura Nowocin, and Abby Brigadoi, who kept me sane during the writing process and were fabulous cheerleaders.

Thanks to Fr. Humbert Kilanowski, O.P., who's always available to answer my theological questions.

Thanks to Sr. Theresa Aletheia Noble, F.S.P., for her beautiful foreword and her constant memento mori inspiration.

To Jaymie Stuart Wolfe, my tireless editor, who dealt with zillions of emails and questions and handled those with good cheer and grace while also editing my manuscript with a deft and sure touch. It is a much better book because of her!

To all the people at Ave Maria Press, who were a joy to work with on this project. I can't imagine a better publishing company or better people to work with!

To Jen Fitz, for rabbits, humor, and pure awesomeness. Without you, this book wouldn't exist.

To my massive extended family. (I'd list y'all, but it would take pages. Seriously.) It's been so much fun doing life with you. Thank you for the millions of prayers, countless care packages, and thousands of celebrations. I'm so lucky to have you!

To Rebecca Frech, Elizabeth Foss, Gina Zeidler, Rhiannon Bosse, Heather Renshaw, and Micaela Darr, who offered advice, prayers, and words of wisdom.

To Tiffany Smith, Amilia Lingel, Tom McGee, Andrea Snyder, Branden Meyer, Troy Baumgardner, Sean O'Connor, Mary Watts, Anne Roberts, and Lindsay Earles, for a lifetime of friendship.

To Sage. I wish you were here to read this, but I have to hope that somehow you're reading it in heaven. Meeting you there will be one of the delights of eternity.

To St. Francis de Sales, patron of writers and the deaf. He worked overtime helping me write this! Credit is also due to St. Thomas Aquinas, St. Elizabeth Ann Seton, the Blessed Mother, St. Mary Magdalene, and St. Catherine of Siena.

And, of course, to our Lord Jesus Christ. I hope to hear you say one day that I wrote well of you, and with St. Thomas Aquinas, I ask for nothing but you.

APPENDIX
A MEMENTO MORI WAY
OF THE CROSS

THE FIRST STATION:
Jesus Is Condemned to Death

We adore you, O Christ, and we praise you.
Because by your holy cross, you have redeemed the world.

Dear Jesus, as you stand before the crowd that is screaming for your blood, your heart must break. You came to save these people, and they reject you only a few days after calling you their king. The adoration of the crowd is fading and fickle. In my own life, the days when I will be completely happy and at peace with the world are also fleeting. One day, I will face death, just as you are. And in that moment, I will need your strength to support me. Increase my sense of your love for me, so that I may live every day with the desire to live my one life to praise and to please you. Help me so that when I face my own death sentence, I can do it with serenity and grace and with the hope of seeing you face-to-face in heaven.

Father, into your hands, I commend my spirit.

THE SECOND STATION:
Jesus Takes Up His Cross

We adore you, O Christ, and we praise you.
Because by your holy cross, you have redeemed the world.

The Cross is now before you, and you still shoulder the burden and begin your walk to Calvary. You are exhausted, Lord, but still, you know this is why you came into the world, to give us abundant life.

As I face my day-to-day trials, help me to remember that your presence makes what you ask me to carry bearable. Remind me that all too soon, my life will end and my chances to live as you would have me live will be gone. Even in dark days, illumine my mind with your love and example, so that I may carry my cross as you carried yours, with an eye on the final goal of heaven and eternal happiness with you.

Father, into your hands, I commend my spirit.

THE THIRD STATION:
Jesus Falls the First Time

We adore you, O Christ, and we praise you.
Because by your holy cross, you have redeemed the world.

As you fall to the ground, Lord, I see myself in you. So often I have fallen and stumbled in my life, letting my worries, griefs, and burdens crush me. So often my cross has seemed too heavy and my problems too insurmountable, and it seems easier to just collapse under their weight and give up.

But you taught me otherwise, Lord. You show me how to get up, even after I fall, and how to embrace the Father's will. Fill me with that same zeal. Give me your strength when mine fails me, so that I can stand and continue on my journey toward you. Help me to die to my selfish desires and sinful actions so that I will become all you created me to be.

Father, into your hands, I commend my spirit.

THE FOURTH STATION:
Jesus Meets His Mother

We adore you, O Christ, and we praise you.
Because by your holy cross, you have redeemed the world.

Seeing your mother must have wrenched your heart, Lord. Yes, she is a familiar, loving face, but oh, the pain she must have felt as she watched you suffer! How you must have wished to take away the tears from her face and remove the sword from her heart!

You needed Mary to encourage you on the path of salvation. You gave me your mother as my own, and in my trials, she gives me strength and hope to continue in this "valley of tears." Thank you for sharing your mother with me. Without her prayers, I could not give myself fully to your plan for my life. Fill me with love for her and enkindle deep devotion to her in my heart, so that I can do whatever you tell me.

Father, into your hands, I commend my spirit.

THE FIFTH STATION:
Simon Helps Jesus Carry His Cross

We adore you, O Christ, and we praise you.
Because by your holy cross, you have redeemed the world.

As Simon helped you, Lord, do not let me refuse the help of others as I journey along my life's path. Keep me from being too proud to accept the help of those who love me and whom you have placed in my life so that I may more perfectly do your will. I am not meant to walk the path alone, Lord. Show me how to walk it with you to the end.

Father, into your hands, I commend my spirit.

THE SIXTH STATION:
Veronica Wipes the Face of Jesus

We adore you, O Christ, and we praise you.
Because by your holy cross, you have redeemed the world.

Here, as I contemplate Veronica's kindness toward you, give me the grace to reach out to help others who are in need. I may only be able to perform a small service to them, but you show me that nothing done with love is ever wasted or "too small" to give. Help me to see beyond my own concerns to the needs of others. Fill me with your vision and your love. Inspire me to do the small things I am able to do before there is no longer any time to do them.

Father, into your hands, I commend my spirit.

THE SEVENTH STATION:
Jesus Falls the Second Time

We adore you, O Christ, and we praise you.
Because by your holy cross, you have redeemed the world.

As you fall the second time, Lord, I am reminded of the times I have sunk to the ground even after rebounding from a previous fall. I was so confident that I would live perfectly and would never fall again. But I have fallen, Lord, and once more I need to look to you. I am not perfect. I am still a work in progress. But never let me stop striving to become what you want me to be, Lord. Do not let me stay mired in discouragement. Instead, give me the grace to rise up, to repent of any sin, and to try again. Someday I will die. I have only this life to do what you ask of me. Give me the desire to press on.

Father, into your hands, I commend my spirit.

THE EIGHTH STATION:
Jesus Meets the Women of Jerusalem

We adore you, O Christ, and we praise you.
Because by your holy cross, you have redeemed the world.

In your pain, Jesus, you could have ignored the women who followed you on the way to your death. Instead, you stopped and spoke to them. In my own pain, keep me from being self-absorbed and selfish. Help me to see past my own suffering and death to the needs of others. Inspire me to act with love, compassion, and gentleness, even when I am distressed.

Father, into your hands, I commend my spirit.

THE NINTH STATION:
Jesus Falls the Third Time

We adore you, O Christ, and we praise you.
Because by your holy cross, you have redeemed the world.

Once again, you fall, Jesus. And once again, my face is in the dust. By now I know that I will continuously fall as I go through my life. But I also know that I must keep moving forward, keep rising toward you, and continue on my path. The cross can seem so heavy, Lord, and the idea of lying down and giving up seems so attractive. But I know that you want more for me, that you have more for me to do. When I have no more strength, Lord, lift me. Help me take the next step, especially when I am exhausted and afraid.

Father, into your hands, I commend my spirit.

THE TENTH STATION:

Jesus Is Stripped of His Garments

We adore you, O Christ, and we praise you.
Because by your holy cross, you have redeemed the world.

You are stripped naked before your tormentors and the jeering crowd. There are times I have felt the same way. People mock me for wanting to live as you ask me to, they taunt me and say you do not exist, that you are just a figment of my imagination. But I know, Lord, that you are a constant, loving, and true presence in my life. In the times when I am embarrassed and humiliated, do not let me disown you. Help me to bear these moments with patience as you did and to follow you faithfully to the end of my life's journey.

Father, into your hands, I commend my spirit.

THE ELEVENTH STATION:
Jesus Is Nailed to the Cross

We adore you, O Christ, and we praise you.
Because by your holy cross, you have redeemed the world.

You surrendered yourself to indescribable pain, Lord, the pain of nails being driven into your flesh, holding you to the instrument of your death. In my own life, I may face physical pain that is beyond my ability to bear or witness the suffering of those I love. I will want to do anything to end that pain. Remind me in these moments to be fastened to you, to offer myself completely to you. Do not allow it to overwhelm me, but help me to remember your suffering and to unite my own with yours. Give me the grace to endure what I must endure.

Father, into your hands, I commend my spirit.

THE TWELFTH STATION:
Jesus Dies on the Cross

We adore you, O Christ, and we praise you.
Because by your holy cross, you have redeemed the world.

You died, Lord, for love. When I come to the end of my earthly life, help me to surrender myself entirely to your will, to place my whole being into your loving hands. Lord, give me the grace to die in your peace and with your name in my heart and on my lips.

Father, into your hands, I commend my spirit.

THE THIRTEENTH STATION:
Jesus Is Taken Down from the Cross

We adore you, O Christ, and we praise you.
Because by your holy cross, you have redeemed the world.

Your broken, battered body is removed from the Cross. Now, the burden of your body is given to your mother and your friends to tend. There are times, Lord, when I feel like a burden to those who love me. I feel their lives would be easier without me, better without me. Help me to see the truth, Lord. You have created me for a specific purpose, and my life is dedicated to fulfilling that purpose. My life and death have value and worth because you created it. Do not let me fall prey to thoughts of despair. Grant me the grace to live courageously, even in the face of fear, and teach me to rest in your arms.

Father, into your hands, I commend my spirit.

THE FOURTEENTH STATION:
Jesus Is Buried

We adore you, O Christ, and we praise you.
Because by your holy cross, you have redeemed the world.

You are laid in the tomb. Your mission on earth, Lord, is over, but mine still goes on. I want to live as you did, completely one with the will of the Father, focused only on his will. Before I am also laid in my tomb, let me live with passion for you. Do not let me waste the time I have on things that do not matter or live for things that are only fleeting and cannot last. Keep my heart focused on what you have called me to, so that, when my life is over, I can go joyfully home to you.

Father, into your hands, I commend my spirit.

THE FIFTEENTH STATION:
Jesus Rises from the Dead

We adore you, O Christ, and we praise you.
Because by your holy cross, you have redeemed the world.

The joy of Easter morning brims over, Lord. You have triumphed over sin, death, despair, and hell! Death shall reign no more!

Lord, I want to see your face forever when I die. I want to bask in the joy of eternal life with you! When things on earth seem difficult, when I am driven to the brink of giving up, inspire me with faith in your resurrection. Show me that death, despair, and sin do not have the last word. Help me to place my life and death in your hands, trusting that you have prepared a place for me to live eternally with you.

Father, into your hands, I commend my spirit.

NOTES

Chapter 1: The End in Sight

1. Richard John Neuhaus, *Death on a Friday Afternoon: Meditations on the Last Words of Jesus from the Cross* (New York: Basic Books, 2000), 80.

2. Dietrich Bonhoeffer, *The Cost of Discipleship* (New York: Touchstone, 2018), 89.

3. *The C. S. Lewis Bible* (San Francisco: HarperOne, 2010), 1123.

Chapter 7: Down Again

1. J. K. Rowling, *Harry Potter and the Deathly Hallows* (New York: Arthur A. Levine Books, 2007), 699.

Chapter 14: Asleep

1. *The C. S. Lewis Bible*, 901.

Epilogue: New Life

1. C. S. Lewis, *The Chronicles of Narnia* (New York: HarperCollins, 2001), 767.

ADDITIONAL RESOURCES

The Examen: the process is explained well at this website: https://www.ignatianspirituality.com/ignatian-prayer/the-examen.

Also helpful is the book *Remember Your Death: Memento Mori Lenten Devotional* by Sr. Theresa Aletheia Noble, F.S.P., and the corresponding journal, *Remember Your Death: Memento Mori Journal*. I've used both, and I use the journal for my nightly Examen. You can purchase both, and read more about Sr. Theresa Aletheia, at her website, https://pursuedbytruth.com.

Emily M. DeArdo is a Catholic writer and speaker who graduated in 2004 from Capital University with a bachelor's degree in political science and English literature. She worked for the Ohio State Senate for ten years. At age eleven, DeArdo was diagnosed with cystic fibrosis, a fatal genetic disease, and she received a double-lung transplant at age twenty-three.

She contributed to several studies published by *Take Up and Read* in 2018 and 2019 and also self-published an eBook, *Catholic 101*. DeArdo has also been a guest on *The Jennifer Fulwiler Show* on SiriusXM Radio. She was named Young Catholic Woman of the Year by the Diocese of Columbus in 2005. She was a contestant on *Jeopardy!* in 2016.

DeArdo, who is a Third Order Lay Dominican, lives in the Columbus, Ohio, area.

Emilymdeardo.com
Facebook: emilymdardowrites
Twitter: @emdeardo
Instagram: @emily_deardo
Pinterest: @emily_m_deardo

Sr. Theresa Aletheia Noble, F.S.P., is the founder of the Memento Mori project and the author of *Remember Your Death: Memento Mori Journal*.